Corvette:

A PIECE OF THE ACTION

IMPRESSIONS OF THE MARQUE AND THE MYSTIQUE

AN AUTOMOBILE QUARTERLY
LIBRARY SERIES BOOK

IMPRESSIONS OF THE MA

BY THE STAFF OF AUTOMO
WITH WILLIAM L. MITC

orvette:
PIECE OF
HE ACTION

RQUE AND THE MYSTIQUE

BILE QUARTERLY MAGAZINE
HELL AND ALLAN GIRDLER

About Automobile Quarterly

AUTOMOBILE *Quarterly* magazine was founded in 1962 as The Connoisseur's Magazine of Motoring Today, Yesterday and Tomorrow. Each issue is filled with 72 to 85 brilliant full-color photographs. A single issue contains between 75,000 and 85,000 words, and many stories are book length. Hardbound like a book, issues contain no advertising to mar your reading pleasure. Automobile Quarterly is indexed and cross-referenced to compose the most comprehensive definitive encyclopedic work on the automobile ever published.

Automobile Quarterly's books on Corvette include: *Corvette: America's Star-Spangled Sports Car* by Karl Ludvigsen; *The Complete Corvette Restoration & Technical Guide—Vol. 1, 1953–1962* by Noland Adams; *Corvette! Thirty Years of Great Advertising* by the staff of Automobile Quarterly; *The Best of Corvette News* edited by Karl Ludvigsen. Other marque histories include: *The Buick: A Complete History* by Terry B. Dunham and Lawrence R. Gustin; *Cadillac: Standard of the World* by Maurice D. Hendry; *Camaro! From Challenger to Champion: The Complete History* by Gary L. Witzenburg; *Chevrolet: A History from 1911* by Beverly Rae Kimes and Robert C. Ackerson; *The Cars That Henry Ford Built* by Beverly Rae Kimes; *Ferrari: The Man, The Machines* edited by Stan Grayson; *Firebird! America's Premier Performance Car: The Complete History* by Gary L. Witzenburg; *General Motors—The First 75 Years* by the editors of Automobile Quarterly; *Mustang! The Complete History of America's Pioneer Ponycar* by Gary L. Witzenburg; *Packard: A History of the Motor Car and the Company* edited by Beverly Rae Kimes; *Porsche: Excellence Was Expected* by Karl Ludvigsen. Additional books include *Automobile Quarterly's World of Cars*; *Great Cars & Grand Marques* edited by Beverly Rae Kimes; *BMW: A History* by Halwart Schrader; *Errett Lobban Cord, His Empire, His Motor Cars: Auburn, Cord, Duesenberg* by Griffith Borgeson; and *Automobile Quarterly's Complete Handbook of Automobile Hobbies* edited by Beverly Rae Kimes.

copyright © 1984 by Princeton Publishing Inc., Princeton, New Jersey 08542—all rights reserved

Typesetting by Kutztown Publishing Company, Kutztown, Pennsylvania; color separations by Graphic Arts Corporation, Toledo, Ohio and Lincoln Graphics, Cherry Hill, New Jersey; printing and binding by South China Printing Co., Hong Kong.

SECOND EDITION

No part of this book may be reproduced or transmitted in any form or by any means, electronic or mechanical, including photocopy, recording, or any information storage and retrieval system now known or to be invented, without permission in writing from the publisher, except by a reviewer who wishes to quote brief passages in a review written for inclusion in a magazine, newspaper or broadcast.

Library of Congress Catalog Number: 84-61085
ISBN 0-915038-44-7: Princeton Publishing Inc.

Automobile Quarterly Publications

PUBLISHER AND EDITOR IN CHIEF:
L. Scott Bailey

EUROPEAN EDITOR:
Griffith Borgeson

ART DIRECTOR:
Michael Pardo

SENIOR EDITOR:
Lowell C. Paddock

ASSISTANT ART DIRECTOR:
David W. Bird II

ASSOCIATE EDITOR:
John F. Katz

CHIEF PHOTOGRAPHER:
Roy Query

PRODUCTION EDITORS:
Cyndy R. Brown, William D. Clark

BUSINESS MANAGER:
Kevin G. Bitz

PRODUCTION ASSISTANT:
Patricia H. Lincoln

CUSTOMER SERVICES:
Donna Wanner

STAFF ASSISTANT:
Margaret Buchanan Bailey

VICE PRESIDENT:
Margaret T. Bailey

BOOK DESIGN:
Theodore R. F. Hall

PORTRAIT PHOTOGRAPHERS:
Rick Lenz, Richard A. Brown, Roy Query

RACING PHOTOGRAPHERS:
Pete Biro, Bill Stahl, Geoffrey Goddard, Rich Chenet
Dave Arnold, J. J. Mollitt, Dwight Pelkin
Stan Rosenthall, Bill Oursler, Norman E. Brust

Contents

Preface to the First Edition

Enthusiasm, the dictionary—in this case, Oxford's unabridged, the third of twelve volumes—tells us, is a word of rather divine origin, denoting in earlier times "possession by a god, supernatural inspiration, prophetic or poetic frenzy." Succeeding centuries brought the meaning down from the rarefied some, to "rapturous intensity of feeling in favour of a person, principle, cause, etc.; passionate eagerness in any pursuit, proceeding from an intense conviction of the worthiness of the object." In either case, it would seem the fellows of The Philological Society, Oxford University and the dictionary editors, the Messrs. Murray, Bradley, Craigie and Onions, somehow—serendipity, prescience, whatever— could have been thinking of nothing other than the very special relationship existing between Man and his Corvette. Since this relationship frequently borders on the spiritual, even the archaic definition applies. Try convincing an impassioned Corvette owner that his car is, after all, merely a compilation of mechanical bits and a quantity of plastic and other human-devised materials, and you've an argument on your hands. The Corvette is more than mortal, more than animate, more than existential. The Corvette is . . . well, a definition just won't do.

Ergo this volume. It is, purely and simply, an enthusiast's book. Thousands of words relating the fervor, hundreds of photographs of the cars that have aroused it. What this book is about is the spirit of the Corvette. It's a logical third book in our Corvette series. Our first volume, *Corvette: America's Star-Spangled Sports Car,* originally published in 1971 and revised and updated in subsequent editions, presented the complete history of the marque. Our second book, *The Best of Corvette News,* published in 1976, was, as its title implies, an anthology of the literature of Corvette. For our third book, we thought it would be fun to get down to the visceral nitty-gritty of it all. And that's what we've done. In text this book presents the impressions of two enthusiasts, one who lived the Corvette story on the inside, who made it happen; one who was a rapt observer on the outside, who watched it happen. The juxtaposition of their vantage points, we thought, might be interesting.

Bill Mitchell was born in Cleveland, raised in Pennsylvania, took himself to New York in the early Thirties and learned how much he really liked cars. At age twenty-three he joined General Motors, moved to Detroit and set about designing cars. Allan Girdler was born in New York City in the middle Thirties, bought his first car at age fourteen (a Model A Ford roadster), and in the mid-Fifties ran away to Oklahoma to become a reporter for the Tulsa *Daily World* and a dedicated member of the sports car movement. Bill created the Corvair, the Riviera, the Grand Prix, the Toronado, the Camaro, the Eldorado, the Firebird . . . the Sting Ray, others too numerous for mention. Allan began writing about such cars—and others, again too numerous for mention—both freelance and as associate editor, later editor, of *Car Life,* executive editor of *Road & Track,* executive editor, and today editor, of *Cycle World.* Bill Mitchell and Allan Girdler. Two worlds linked only by subject, it would seem. But markedly akin when the subject is a Corvette—as this book reveals. Tell us what it was like, we asked them both.

The enthusiastic written word is but part of the Corvette saga presented here. In photographs it represents more Corvettes than we've had the time to count. Production cars, experimental cars, racing cars, custom cars, you name it. What perhaps is most fascinating about the Corvette is the very large world it encompasses. A Corvette is simply not a car that comes off the assembly line, is loaded off to somewhere and thereafter driven home by its new owner to remain in selfsame image and be utilized only to get from here to there. It's more than that, much more—as has already been suggested. Some owners of vintage Corvettes have gone to painstaking lengths to return the car to exact factory specs and, figuratively, the clothes it wore when Harley Earl or Bill Mitchell designed it. Others have worked equally hard to fashion the Corvette to their own individual image, much like Bill Mitchell himself does with his personal cars. Both sorts of Corvettes are presented here, both sorts of Corvettes are very much part of the Corvette story. Those Corvettes which represent only a minor deviation from the norm are noted as "owner modified." The all-out custom variations will, of course, be easily recognized. Likewise the racing cars—and the dragsters, another breed of Corvette that is dashing, to say the least.

For all these varied cars, we've used the talents of a number of people from, literally, coast to coast. Rick Lenz, our indefatigable photographer in the West, spent months snapping shutters for us along the Pacific and in the desert. Richard Brown piled his Cambo 4x5 and related equipment in his van and trekked the South on our behalf. Roy Query took his camera to more cities and hamlets in the Midwest than he heretofore had known existed.

Many photographers, too, energetically dug deep into their color files or ran to the races to produce the Corvette competition coverage which is included herein: Pete Biro, Bill Stahl, J. J. Mollitt, Geoffrey Goddard, Dave Arnold, Stan Rosenthall, Dwight Pelkin, Bill Oursler, Norman E. Brust. Assisting Allan Girdler with research, background and recollections were Sonya Keith, Bob D'Olivo, Wayne Thoms and Anatole Arutunoff—and for the rudiments, the raw material, Allan had the help of Dick Guldstrand, Dick Durant, as well as familial assistance from Reynolds and Tad Girdler, father and brother respectively. Most supportive of all was Lynn Girdler who, as Allan writes, "has sat through more races, more hours in a tow car and more hours of not interrupting while I type than any human being should be asked to endure."

Cheerfully lending their Corvette expertise to our photographers were David Duggan, Vic Feldon, Bill Kluss and Don Rood on the West Coast. In the Midwest, we had Becky Bodnar, Bob Daniels, Dave Densmore and Jay Lamka; in the East, Chip Miller; in the South, Bill Locke. Bill, associate editor of *Vette Vues* and Corvette enthusiast extraordinaire, also provided valuable assistance to the editor in production car verification.

Helping the editor immeasurably as well as the author of *Corvette: America's Star-Spangled Sports Car,* the compiler of *The Best of Corvette News,* AQ contributing editor, a good friend and valued colleague—all in the person of Karl Ludvigsen. A number of years ago an administrative aide to the President commented that he slept better nights knowing Lyndon Johnson was in the White House. The remark was frequently quoted, oft jocularly. That—and politics—notwithstanding, one might paraphrase that the advice, counsel and support of Karl on the subject of Corvette is more tranquilizing to the editorial psyche than Valium, and assuredly more pleasant to take.

And in Detroit, where the Corvette was born and where its present and future is decided, we had the good help of a number of people in Chevrolet Motor Division: Floyd Joliet, Dick Henderson, Frank Moelich, Dave Holls, Bob Lund, Chuck Jordan, Bob Vint, Dave McLellan, Jim Williams, Jim Israel, Gloria Jezewski, Sybil DeKeyser.

Many people, then, had a part in the realization of this book. Our thanks to them all for their contributions, without which, as the cliché goes, this volume would not have been possible. We are grateful to them for another reason. We've had a good time. Putting together this book has been fun. But then, that's what the Corvette is all about.

Beverly Rae Kimes
Editor, First Edition

Princeton, New Jersey

Preface to the Second Edition

It was on my way home from school one March afternoon in 1968 that I first took note of the gleaming Nassau blue '66 Sting Ray convertible at the local Chevy dealer. Corvettes had always seized my eye, but this particular car stirred up raw passion. The following Saturday I dragged my reluctant father down to the dealer's lot to show him my find. Two days later, in return for a 1965 Buick Skylark and $2650, the Corvette was his. After almost twenty years it's still in the garage. Being driven daily has led to some problems with rust: one day the frame, filled with disease, let go of the rear axle. But my father refuses to buy something more practical; nothing can match the almighty roar of the 327 with all its barrels opened up. At an age when many men look forward to a pleasant game of golf, he looks forward to the first day of spring when he can throw down the top, throw on his cap and know that he will turn heads. And that, in a nutshell, is the essence of Corvette ownership, and what has made the car such an important part of the American psyche and marketplace since 1953. In the previous edition of *A Piece of the Action,* we left off in 1978, a time when many feared that the Corvette would be extinguished by either the economy, the government or the cost of fuel. But, with the enthusiasm of fans inside and outside of Chevrolet, the Corvette hung on. In 1984, it received a new breath of life, with overdue styling and engineering updates. A new generation of Corvettes had begun. To chronicle the progress of the Corvette since 1978, we turned again to author Allan Girdler, whose affection for and knowledge of Corvettes allowed him to pick up where he left off. Assisting us along the way were Joe Hicks, Joe Tori, Ralph Kramer and Jim Rooney of Chevrolet who helped us to photograph the new Corvettes. Also instrumental in preparing the second edition was associate editor John Katz, who handled all the revisions, large and small. Special thanks are due to all the Corvette owners who volunteered their cars. Theirs is a special devotion.

Lowell C. Paddock
Editor, Second Edition

Princeton, New Jersey

The Corvette Sag

William L. Mitchell talks about how the Corvette came to

You know the difference between a shark and a grouper? You see them both in the water. The shark is nervous, intense, active, rapacious, a fusiform body, lateral gills, fins, lots of things to look at. A big grouper just lies there, fat and satisfied. It's John Barrymore's profile against Churchill's. A greyhound and a bulldog. A sports car and a sedan.

You know the great thing about a sports car? When you're designing it, you can put your arms around it. You can't do that with a family sedan. It's a very emotional thing.

It might never have happened for me. My dad was a small-town Buick dealer in Pennsylvania; he'd get a Stutz or a Mercer in trade and he'd soup them up, customize them. He had four different Bearcats over the years. I'd probably be a Buick dealer today, hotting up somebody else's cars instead of my own—except for the Colliers.

It was 1927, my fifteenth birthday, and I landed a job in New York City with the Barron Collier agency as an office boy in the art department. I worked there during my summer vacations and upon graduation from high school I started full time as a layout man and illustrator. To improve my skills as an artist, I attended night school classes at the Art Students League in 1931 and 1932. Lunch-hours I spent along 57th Street and in the showrooms displaying such beauteous European road machines as Isotta-Fraschini, Hispano-Suiza, Rolls-Royce and Mercedes-Benz. I can still see one of those chassis sitting there, just the chassis, brightly chromed with red wire wheels—for $8500.

While at the Barron Collier agency, I worked up the first M.G. ads in America, but it was my association with Collier's sons, particularly Sam and Miles, that really got me turned on to sports cars. They brought European road racing back to this country in the Thirties, using the long driveways of Overlook, the family estate in Pocantico Hills, for their course initially. I'd go up there and race with them, and make sketches. I designed the badge and blazer patch for their Automobile Racing Club of America, which presaged the SCCA, but

most memorably I drove—and found out

what driving was all about. Those foreign sports cars, they would go like hell over a gravel road. The fun with the car was to almost lose it, I mean to always drive on that narrow edge. No windshield, a cut-down door. It was you and four wheels. You felt every twitch, everything the car was doing. The M.G. Magnettes, the Amilcars, the Rileys, the Bugattis. That Ettore Bugatti was incredible, he built a car with practically no suspension—of course, there wasn't much of that in any of the sports cars in those days—but the sexy look of a Bugatti would drive you crazy. And I drove like crazy. One of these cars, and then another, and then another. I wished to God the United States had something like them.

In the summer of 1935, an insurance executive by the name of Walter Carey attended one of the Collier competitions at Sleepy Hollow Ring. He saw some of my sketches depicting the races and asked me if I had ever thought about designing cars. He said he was a personal friend of Harley Earl, who was director of all General Motors styling, and wanted to send him some of my work. Mr. Earl responded with a letter from his business manager, Howard O'Leary, asking me to develope some design sketches. I worked all summer creating a stack of new ideas and sent them off in the fall of 1935. Before Christmas I was asked to come to Detroit, and on December 15th, 1935, I joined General Motors.

It was a big break—and, initially, a mixed blessing. Although my work at General Motors was exciting, I soon missed the thrill of sports car racing and the many hours I used to spend at Zumbach's sports car garage on the west side of Manhattan. The sports car, so far as Detroit was concerned, was just vague terminology for a machine that no one comprehended, nor cared to.

By the fall of 1936, I was made chief designer of the Cadillac Studio, a rather quick promotion, you might say, which perhaps it was, although GM's entire Art and Color Section had less than a hundred people then, including the fabrication shop. My first big assignment was the design of the 1938 '60' Special. Intended as a LaSalle, it

emerged as the first "youth image" Cadillac. It was an interesting challenge but it wasn't really what I wanted to do.

About that time, I tried to talk GM into giving me a leave of absence so I could join Mercedes for a while. To me, there were no American race cars—Indianapolis and all those funny-looking high roadsters didn't stir me at all. But in Europe, Mercedes and Auto Union were having their great duels, and I wanted to be there and be part of it. I wanted to drive one of those incredible cars, it was my burning ambition. General Motors said no.

So I stayed home and devoured every issue of *Autocar*, drooling over the racing paintings of Gordon Crosby, and reading every other foreign journal I could get my hands on—and suffering the strange looks of everyone around Detroit who really didn't know what I was about. Except Harley Earl. He had a feeling for cars. Once, in '41, when I was on the West Coast, he took me around Los Angeles, 120 or 130 miles, from one shop to another, to see what was happening. You'd chase a guy up the street, follow him into his garage, and look at what he had done—special headrests, cut-down bodies, the whole works. I went nuts that day. Tommy Lee—his late father was the famous coachbuilder Don Lee—inspired me the most. His shop was cluttered with Delages, Talbots, a Cord with Miller race engine, I don't know how many Frontenac Fords, everything different, built from the ground up—and then taken to Lake Muroc for some competition. Fantastic. Four guys would build four cars and then go up to Muroc to prove who was the fastest.

There was nothing like that in Detroit, *nothing*! It existed on the West Coast and the East. But not in Detroit. I'm not sure, maybe it's simply that Detroit is too close to the automobile. By that I mean, if you work in a candy store, more than likely you soon get tired of candy. And they tell me that few bartenders drink. Well, very few top executives in the industry love automobiles. Bunkie Knudsen loved cars, Harlow Curtice loved cars . . . now I'm running out. The others love business, and the business just happens to be cars. I'm not really criticizing, they're good at what they do, they just don't comprehend an automobile as anything other than the particular segment of the transportation industry in which they're engaged.

I recall once we were down in São Paulo and I had a chance to take a three-liter Maserati around the Interlagos track with a test driver from GM do Brasil who was called the Fangio of Brazil. I gave that car a hell of a ride. Really enjoyed it, though the thing was throwing oil. I arrived back at the hotel pretty messy. Where have you been, GM's top executive asked me? Out at the test track driving some cars. What happened? The car was throwing oil. Well, don't we have windshields? Then he asked me how fast I was going. I don't know, I said, because there's no speedometer on a race car. What do you mean? I said there's a tach on it and you do so many rpm's and you shift at certain speeds. He said oh. They'll never understand.

Somehow, despite years of this sort of thing, there emerged the Corvette.

Bill with his first Corvette racer, the SR-2; and his Sting Ray as a show car in post-competition days.

Persistence I guess.

A good designer has got to be creative, and to be creative you've got to be dissatisfied and discontent. It makes for a terrible personality. And there are two things you've got to know how to do as a designer. You've got to know when to have enough guts to follow through and not give up and, on the other hand, when to quit and turn around. To say stop it, that's not right. I've changed the colors on Corvettes, had them repainted at the last minute. But I never changed my mind about the Corvette idea.

There's one more thing about a designer—at least in today's world—he has to put up with committees. Do you recall that scene in *The Hucksters* where Sidney Greenstreet stood up, spit on the board room table, and said, "now you remember that!"? Well, that's kind of what I've been doing for the past quarter century. I suspect a lot of people have thought I might mellow somewhere along the line, but I haven't . . . and never will. I say what I think. And I think the committee approach to automobile design is . . . well, what I think is

spired in Bimini, designed in Detroit, and a sensation at the New York show in '62, the Mako Shark I.

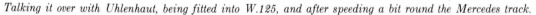

Talking it over with Uhlenhaut, being fitted into W.125, and after speeding a bit round the Mercedes track.

unprintable. And that says it.

The financial people—bean counters we like to call them—need an attractive, well designed product before they can count their beans. The sales people need something aesthetically saleable in order to sell. The engineers need a good design too, how successful would their work be without it? I'm not a bean counter, I'm not a salesman, I'm not an engineer. I'm a designer, and I like cars that look like they should be driven. Try explaining that to a committee. If you go to a good tailor, if you're smart, you don't tell him how to make a suit, you say "make a suit for me; you do it, you know how to do it." Likewise an automobile designer. Our biggest problem at Design Staff is that most divisional general managers feel that they have to pick all the designs for their new models. Just because a man is an outstanding engineer or salesman doesn't mean that he has good taste or a sense of design.

Nothing infuriates me more than a bunch of guys from sales or engineering or whatever taking a look at one of my cars and then going off to a corner to whisper. Take this off, don't do that, we can't do this. When that happens, I go off to a corner of my own and do my own car. Studio X is what we call

it, and it's a refuge. Harley Earl always had a special car going somewhere—and so have I, sometimes several. Once there was the Sting Ray, the Manta Ray, the two Monzas and I don't know what else. There's something there all the time. I do it for myself—and if it works, I borrow off of it and put it on something else. Or I just take it and let it sit down in the garage. And as some of the general managers walk by, they'll say, "Wow! Let me have that one. Let's produce it!"

That was how we did the first Riviera back in the early Sixties. Trying to explain a new concept in automobile design to a committee is next to impossible. You have to demonstrate what you mean by actually building the car. That's the best way to do it, your way . . . and then see what happens. You can line up any group of cars from the past to the present and I'll bet I can tell you which ones were committee designed and which ones were left to the designer. For example, the first Camaro introduced in 1967 never had strong identity. Too many fingers were in the pie when it was designed. The present Firebird and Camaro were never touched by a committee prior to their introduction in 1970. They were done

completely by designers and done in a hurry . . . that's good design . . . and today they're classics.

And then there's market research. You can ask somebody where you've been, but not where you're going. Frank Lloyd Wright didn't go around ringing doorbells asking people what kind of houses they wanted. And I'm sure Hattie Carnegie didn't stop women on the street and question them about the kind of hats they liked. The top fashion designers in Paris don't walk up and down the Champs Elysees asking every woman how she prefers her skirts or what's her favorite neckline; they dictate the fashions and people love it. That's what a designer must do. He must have the ability to look ahead and visualize new trends. Designing is a profession that requires good taste and judgment. A designer can't fall in love with this year's designs, he has to have an eye and ear to the future. A designer has to have imagination to visualize tomorrow. And everyone knows how hard it is to sell a fur coat in July or a straw hat in January.

My way has never involved market research. What a lot of bull. I really bounce those guys. A while back they made a big survey out in Houston, fastback versus

hatchback, and it showed the hatchback to be the thing. So, I'm sitting in this engineering policy meeting—and they're setting up this graph. I like to be controversial, as most everybody knows. To refine my terminology, I suggested the survey was a bunch of the stuff horses leave behind on parade routes. Everybody looked up. "Why the hell did you run a survey in Houston unless it was on saddles and horses," I said. "I've just come from Paris, there wasn't a hatchback there, that's where the styles come from." Blew a hundred thousand dollar survey right out of the water. Just like that.

There isn't a good-looking car I ever did that market research had anything to do with. And market research never touched the Corvette—never. I shudder to think what would have happened to it if it had.

Actually, with regard to the Corvette, we were left pretty much alone. I guess the bigwigs recognized that they didn't understand the car—though once when I made some crack about advanced age and sports cars not exactly going hand in hand, GM chairman Donner did quickly point out to me that he had gotten more than one Corvette for his friends over sixty. In any case, we weren't bothered much.

Harley Earl has to be given a lot of credit. He came from Hollywood, he'd seen the same things I'd seen, he really wanted to have a sports car. That first one was shown at our proving ground for a board of directors show. He had hidden it, unveiled it and just said, well, what do you think of this? There was quite a little enthusiasm but, of course, those guys weren't sports car drivers. Then Harley got it in the New York show and a lot of people saw it—and the enthusiasm was such that it had to built.

Harley Earl named it Corvette after the small, highly maneuverable Canadian warship used during the Second World War. This name met the requirements for Chevrolet at that time by starting with the letter "C." At first, many of us didn't like the name, but there's a funny thing about names.

Many years ago, for example, I disliked the name "Pontiac," because I never liked the car. Pontiacs were always gorped-up, they were all "committee designed" cars. The Pontiac image was rather like that of an old maid.

One night I got into a discussion at the Pierre Marquette Road and Gun Club with Colin Campbell, who handled the Pontiac account at the time. He said, "If the car was any good, the name would be good. Look at the name Duesenberg . . . that could be the name of a sausage, but the car was so great that the phrase 'It's a Duesie' still signifies fine quality." By contrast, the Edsel was such a flop that the name conjures up visions of a dumb, awkward, clumsy-looking loser.

When Bunkie Knudsen took over Pontiac, he came to Harley Earl and said, "I want hot cars; I want to get the suspenders off the hood and change this image into something that will sell." With the designs that followed, we did manage to turn Pontiac's image around. Knudsen's engineers got the horsepower up and away it went! Pontiac overnight passed Buick and Olds, and wound up in third place behind Ford. The split-grille front end really started something new. There wasn't anything on the road like it. This is what we were striving to do. And, today, Pontiac still has this image.

The 1954 Corvette looked great, but was a weak performer. Pretty is as pretty does, and that first Corvette was pretty is. Its six-cylinder engine was not exactly what you would expect in a sleek-looking sports car. Fortunately, along came the V-8 and Zora and we beat some Jags and Mercedes at Elkhart Lake and Watkins Glen, and when that happened, boy, the Corvette became something! We were really inspired then. We made various changes in the car, and Harley let me build my first racer—the SR-2. Then Harley retired in 1958, I was given his job—and the Corvette was my baby.

By this time, I was rarin' to go. Peter Helck, whose work I'd always admired, stopped by to see me one day and we talked racing. He said two interesting things. First, that there wasn't a racing composition he'd ever done during the painting of which he didn't feel he was driving the car he was drawing. Walter Gotschke, and he's tops too, must do his stuff the same way. You've just got to feel it, to capture what it's like. And second, Peter said, why the devil isn't GM racing? I had the answer for that, I didn't like it, but I had the answer. Harlow Curtice had been head of the National Safety Council, it wouldn't look good, so Chevrolet had stopped racing. Then I took Peter downstairs to see a special project of mine. He loved it. I called it Sting Ray.

Impatient now that the '63 Sting Ray Corvette was reality, Bill began work immediately on the car that would leave 'em gasping in the mid-Sixties, Mako Shark

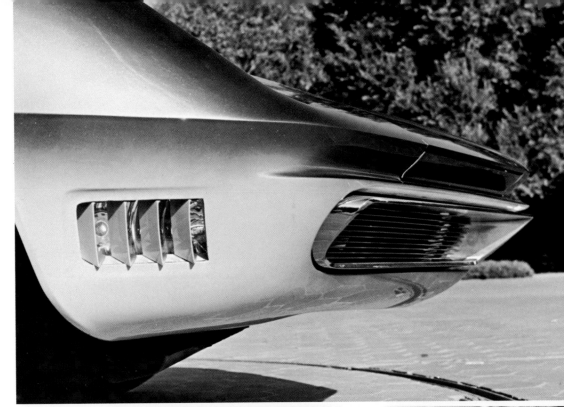

By now—late 1958—Curtice had retired, John Gordon was GM president, Ed Cole head of Chevrolet, and there wasn't any longer a National-Safety-Council/good-appearances reason that we couldn't race. Chevrolet had a racing chassis it no longer needed, and I talked Ed Cole into letting me have it at a good price, with the understanding that I'd sell it back to GM when I finished with it. So I designed a body and hired a guy in Chevrolet Engineering to put it together in our hammer room in the basement during his off-hours and on weekends. During its first outing, at Marlborough, with Dick Thompson aboard, its twin servo braking system acted up. Dick couldn't handle it, one wheel locked, than another—we led for a while but there was no way we could win with that brake problem. We finished fourth, and John Gordon heard about it. You shouldn't be racing, he said, stop it. With the help of some of my designers, I drafted a nice letter back saying that racing with the Colliers and the sketches I had done for them was the very reason I had been invited to join GM, that racing was in my blood. Permission was granted—so long as I didn't spend any of GM's money and didn't keep the car on the premises. That was easy enough. I rented a garage off 12 Mile Road, and the Sting Ray was raced by Dick Thompson for the next two years at all the famous tracks in the country—Elkhart Lake, Laguna Seca, Riverside, Danville—and did really well. I paid all the bills, had to negotiate with the government for a while but got a decent deal on my income tax. Finally John Gordon said enough was enough and to put an end to it, which was perhaps just as well; I might have ended up in bankruptcy court otherwise.

General Motors obviously has the money for competition; I've always thought they should use it. We've had some hairy Corvettes that never got out. And the competition cars, I wish to hell they had let us race them. Those cars weren't even tried. It's a shame. We built a mid-engine car a few years ago that I'd love to try out. It's a beauty . . . it's the Aerovette.

I keep my own foot in, however. Any chance I can get. Back in '58 Rudi Uhlenhaut let me take W.125 out on the Mercedes track near Stuttgart. It was a twenty-year-old dream come true. The hood a block long, twenty-inch wheels, a big blower . . . I got in and put the steering wheel on, and went round and round. It was raining. My idol Rudi Caracciola was the rain master. I thought, god, I'll never get this chance again, I've got to find out how it worked. When Caracciola came into a corner, instead of braking, he'd floor it, the blower would come on and those twenty-inch wheels would take that beast right around. So I tried it . . . more than once. It worked, beautifully. Suddenly there were Mercedes all over the track, with their lights on. Mitchell, they thought, was going to go over the wall. When I brought her in, Uhlenhaut came over

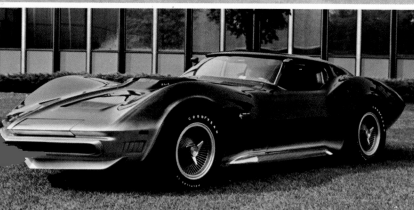

A man's home, they say, is his castle. In Bill Mitchell's case, his castle is his garage wherein are housed his very special cars—or his trophy room wherein are gathered his memories of a sporting life, memorabilia and the portraits he commissioned from M. Olbres and D. North of racing drivers he's known and admired, and race scenes painted by Walter Gotschke. And Bill's driveway has frequently been visited by many of the other cars shown on these pages. Bill Mitchell enjoys driving his cars as much as creating them.

Above, from far left: The Manta Ray, restyled from Mako Shark II for the show season of 1969; XP-882 which had its New York debut in 1970; the 2-Rotor first shown to the public in Frankfurt, Germany in September 1973; and the 4-Rotor which joined it in Paris for the salon in October of '73. Left: The Aero Coupe show car of 1969, many styling details of which were incorporated on the 1970 production car. Right: The Sirocco, a design evaluation on a '68 production car. Pages following: The striking Astro-Vette of '68.

and said I needn't have worried, that he had doctors there. I wasn't worried and I figured the doctors had to be there for the car anyway, not me.

I digress, but that ride was some digression. I drove a 300 SL Gullwing there too, in '55; I still think it's one of the best cars Mercedes ever built. We had plans for a Gullwing of our own about then but everything showed it too heavy. Now we could do it, and I think we should. We've a couple of Gullwing Corvettes around already that we could turn for production.

That's the fun of a sports car. There's so damned much you can do with it to make it exciting, you're not constricted, you've got the freedom of knowing that what you do isn't destined to be used for a car pool. There's only one restriction really, you've got to have people who know sports cars designing them. And I've had a great bunch of guys working for me, from the beginning—Clare MacKichan, Irv Rybicki, Hank Haga, Dave Holls, Chuck Jordan, Jerry Palmer. They have gasoline in their blood. That's what has made the Corvette successful. Every one of my guys drives a Corvette, and other sports cars, Ferraris, Maseratis, Jags, you name it. They talk cars. They live cars.

Michaelangelo didn't paint the whole Sistine Chapel by himself, he had a lot of help, but he was directing the show. Frank

The motorcycling Mitchell, always suited to match.

Lloyd Wright, if you worked for him, you had his religion. My guys think like I do; I don't have to bully them. I dispatch what I want, they carry it out, they don't need me. If it gets off track, I'll get it back on. It's a personal thing, it has to be, I don't want anything to leave my place that isn't what I believe in. They know that, so I don't have to dictate. It isn't necessary. I'll let them run their own meetings with management. I won't attend. But if they're not winning, they'll step to the phone and call me—and I'll come in slugging. Most of the time I win. Not always.

There was the matter of a four-seater Corvette to be introduced in 1963 following the Sting Ray models, an idea whose time, one hopes, shall never come. Harry Barr, who was chief engineer of Chevrolet, was on my side, he didn't want to do it. It was Ed Cole's notion. He made me get the windshield high enough so a four-passenger could be made out of the two-seater. You can't do that. You either make a two-seater, or a four-seater. Otherwise you have a bastard really. The four-seater idea was eventually dropped, and we had a two-seater that looked stocky as hell. Ah, well.

A battle or two may have been lost along the way, but the war's been won. We still have the Corvette. Dear god, a few years ago Roche wanted to wash the car out. The money wasn't coming out right. We had a

hell of a go-round with it. Corvette's got greater owner loyalty than any other car in America, I argued, it's one thing we've got that Ford hasn't. I said, "Jim, if you don't go to the races, you don't see any of this. If you were at Elkhart Lake, you'd see two or three hundred cars that these kids love. And General Motors is going to say we won't make them anymore." It was incredible.

It's the kids I care about. They know what the Corvette is all about. The Corvette is you, whoever you are. After I mounted that shark I caught at Bimini, I kept looking at it on the wall, and I said I'm going to make a car look like that. It wasn't one specific thing about it, it was the whole—the blue body with the white belly, the shimmery silver that was picked up when the sun hit it. I just had to have that car. And after the Mako Shark, there was the Manta Ray devilfish. I saw a Corvette in it too.

And that's what the Corvette owners do. They see the car as a vehicle of personal expression, an extension of themselves, a car that is individually their own. Whenever I go to a Corvette Corral, I recognize this. I'm all for the customizing of a Corvette. Lots of times when it's known I'll be attending one of these events, I'll get a call or two, somebody wants to bring out a pet Corvette and show me what he's done. That's one reason we may have to keep to fiberglass for Corvettes. It lends itself so readily to change.

Bill's Corvette Mulsanne, and the Harley Davidson for which he designed a body that's nicely far-out.

In a way a Corvette is never really finished. There's always something you can do. You've got to wear it, and after you've worn it a while, you'll find things you can do to make it more your own, more comfortable to you. How long now have I had the Shark? I still drive it home every night, along back roads so I can play a little bit. And the Manta Ray and racing Sting Ray are years old; every year I'm doing something, fixing the pedals, arranging the wheel, fixing the seat, so that when I take those babies around, boy, it's me. The kids do that too.

And the wild paint jobs, the fun, the humor that you can bring to the Corvette—I enjoy seeing that. My wife had a white one, I painted eyelashes on it.

That's another thing about the kids—and I use that term less chronologically than as a state of mind. The kids now include a lot of

girls. There must be six secretaries in my office alone who are Corvette owners. And a girl in a Corvette is something special. She might look good in a Camaro, sure, but in a Corvette, well it's just a little bit different. I'll always wave at a girl in a Corvette. More than likely, she'll wave at me first.

I've a little eleven-year-old daughter who would, I think, drive a Stingray up and down the driveway all day if she was allowed to. She knows cars. Once I saw a sports car in the distance and pointed it out to her as the new Ferrari. She said, "Dad, that's the new Corvette." It's embarrassing to be corrected by an eleven year old . . . about your own car. But I had never seen it on the road, only in the studio, and there's a difference. As Ernie Seaholm, the old chief engineer at Cadillac, said, a car in a studio is like a horse in the kitchen. It's a motion product, you've

got to see it out with other cars. We can look at them here, they're all approved, the 1979's are gone as far as I'm concerned, and the 1980's are well along. But until they're on the road for a while, mixing it up with the other cars, you don't really know whether they'll wear well or not. Traditionally, I think, a Corvette has worn well.

Styling is an evolutionary thing. We all tried to out-fin each other back in the Fifties, and we let the fat look get out of hand in the Sixties and early Seventies, when the industry got so carried away with turn-under and tumblehome that some of the cars started looking like horseshoe crabs on roller skates. That wouldn't go now. The times have changed. I must admit that I'm not enthusiastic about all the trends in contemporary design. Some cars look like six guys did them, and they all had their own

Pages preceding and these pages: Currently making the rounds of the automobile shows and the Corvette of the future according to Bill, the breathtaking Aero-Vette.

way. The folded paper school of design as propounded in some Turin studios leaves me cold, and I abhor the subjugation of beauty and elegance to function. A dumb-looking box is a dumb-looking box, no matter how utilitarian it is. You can't have a car so simple there's nothing to look at. That's simple like in Simon. A car has to have enough interest so that it looks different each time you glance at it, each time you see it you see a little more. That's what a Corvette should always be.

There are a few things it won't be in the future, however. One of them is big. The soon-to-come Corvette, I'd say, will be very close to Pininfarina's new Ferrari 308 GTB, we're closing in on that package size. And the big engine will be gone too. Nobody's crying too much about that, at least I'm not. I remember when Mercedes went from some

six liters down to one and a half, showed up at Tripoli and ran the tail off everybody. No, the changes that will come won't ruin our car. It will still be a Corvette, it will just be a tighter car.

What I'd personally like to see for the Corvette is one trim quality, make it the best, the epitome of high style, and sell the car for twelve or fifteen thousand. I don't think we could make enough of them. And why not try building the Corvette in some of our plants overseas for the European market? So far as I'm concerned, unless something now unforeseen happens, the hot sports cars for the next ten years will come from three factories: Ferrari, Porsche—and Corvette.

I'll be watching. I'll be as fascinated a spectator as everybody else who is interested in high performance cars. By the time this reaches print, I'll have retired from General

Motors, after forty years. Retired? Bad word. I'll still be doing much the same thing I've always enjoyed doing: cutting up cars, changing them, making them hotter—I've got a Pontiac Firebird now with a Ferrari Daytona engine in it. I call it Pegasus. And I've got my motorcycles, I've been designing them for a while now. They're my latest passion; with a car you're in the wagon and the horse is up front, but when you ride a bike, you're the horse . . . It's a great feeling. You don't pick your nose when you ride a bike. Of course, I don't recommend that when you drive a Corvette either.

You can look for me in the Corvette Corrals, at the hot rod and custom shows. I'll be there. As long as there's a Corvette on four wheels, a hot bike on two, that I can do something with, I'll stay young. No doubt about that.

Back home astride one of the nine motorcycles in his collection, and down in Daytona, properly suited and properly serious, discussing things before the races.

The Corvette Saga

Recounted by Allan Girdler, who w
power, brutal speed, more car tha

In the

How they did it right, I don't know. Corvette has been, is now, and likely always will be America's only true sports car. You can make a good case for its being the best complete high performance car and the best touring car as well. But it's more than that, too. No car made anywhere in the world can exceed Corvette when it comes to owner loyalty and enthusiasm. Around this core of extreme devotion is a, literally, world-wide appeal. Age and gender and nationality pose no barriers. If a human being likes cars, odds are he or she, at one time or another, wanted to own a Corvette.

All this comes from a corporation whose success is largely based on treating its product, the motorcar, as a product—and from a division within that corporation with a reputation, until our story begins anyway, for turning out cars with a stodge factor of about forty percent. A nickname like Stovebolt doesn't summon up for one an image of flashing innovation.

Timing? Corvette made its own timing. Faith? The faithful were few and far between, similarly tepid was the backing of Generous Mother. Planning? The Corvette didn't seem to be planned, or perhaps the plan was one thing and the car became something else.

The clearest factor here is that the casual orthodox history of Corvette, and the sports car movement of which Corvette was a part, doesn't say it all. At least to those of us who were watching it happen.

There are two orthodoxies. The eastern version says that just after World War II an unspecified number of ex-servicemen came home with M.G.'s they'd seen and admired in England. Their friends saw the cars and bought more, which in turn exposed the whole idea to other daring young men who bought cars of their own and boom! all of a sudden there was a market for sports cars and Detroit, with General Motors leading, got into the sports car thing.

The western version has a few terribly skilled club racers lurking on the winding roads of Southern California. They zip out and dice with men driving, oh, Fords and Chevies and Hudsons. The domestic product

takes a jolly good thrashing and the owners search until they find an exotic dealership where they can buy one of those amazing little cars from across the Atlantic water.

Neat. Tidy. Both versions make lovely stories and probably the first man to write them down believed them, as did the other scribes who've been repeating them into gospel for nearly thirty years. But the sports car didn't arrive exactly like that. Oh, there surely were a few M.G.'s brought home from England and surely at least one homesick Englishman played jack-the-bear with any Ford-driving gulls he could find, but think of the time lag. Even in an age of instant and inescapable communication, it takes years for an idea to spread. How long from whence the Beatles and their funny haircuts arrived until a President could have his hair over his ears? Take away television and the gossip magazines, the talk shows, the youth market and there's no way you can bring in a score of M.G. TC's in 1947, have Chevrolet answer with the Corvette in 1953 and a mushroom of atomic proportion immediately follow, unattended by sociological factors. To wit.

We must also have people waiting for the idea whose time has come. Daring young men of means brought in M.G.'s and other imports, sporting and racing, all during the Twenties and Thirties. There were professional and amateur road races during the Great Depression, not just for the wealthy sportsmen but for top pros as well. But the great public said "That's a cute little car you got there," and went right on saving so they could move from a four to a six to an eight, from flapping side curtains to all-steel bodies with radio, heater and automatic transmission.

No. The mass sports car movement and the Corvette came from something else, from a support base both wider and less easily defined than the spindly little M.G.'s.

Begin with Depression ended by War ended by Peace and Prosperity. Technical progress is war's only useful product. Suddenly there were entire populations ready and willing to do something different, mostly enjoy themselves. Somehow, in some mysterious way no one of us really

From the Outside

atched it happen, who likes sheer
h he needs – who likes Corvettes

Beginning

understands, we became interested in driving cars for the fun of it—and it is fun, no doubt about that.

Here is this vague willingness floating about, then, looking for objects to fill it. There was a boomlet, true, in that in response to these invisible signals there came M.G.'s, Singers, Rileys, Jaguars, Porsches, Simcas, Bandinis, Siatas, D.B.'s, from all manner of countries and in all sorts of forms.

Everybody knew everybody wanted to have fun driving.

Nobody knew exactly what car everybody wanted to drive.

Which is why we had all those funny little coupes and roadsters and overstuffed convertibles and elegant barges. We had Crosley Hotshot parked near Willys Jeepster and Nash-Healey. Plymouth had a two-seat roadster and England sent us the Armstrong-Siddeley Sapphire, a name and title which still makes me giggle. Had a lump of an

engine and a transmission unmatched for complexity and refusal to work right . . . never mind.

The point is, about the time the friends of those elusive ex-GI's first peered under that long hood at that silly little foreign engine, the smart men at Chevrolet began working on a sports car.

In retrospect it's easy to snicker and that isn't fair. Automatic transmissions were dream material back then, so they gave the Corvette an automatic. The M.G. came with a long-in-the-tooth passenger-car engine hotted up with twin carbs, so the Corvette got the Stovebolt Six with three carbs. Somebody must have seen rock guards over headlights on some manner of sporting machine, so they went on the Corvette. The car became a roadster, with side curtains and flimsy top. The styling had more swoop than anything Chevy had ever done. And the material was fiberglass, at that time a daring

step for Chevrolet and as close to space age as anything on the market. All we knew about fiberglass then was that all prophets said soon everything would be made of plastic, which then didn't have the derogatory meaning it has in some quarters now.

Side and snide note: Back about this time *Consumer Reports* recommended the VW Beetle as an alternative for the man who wanted sports car performance with family convenience. Obviously there wasn't much unanimity in America regarding what a sports car was all about.

Ah, that first Corvette. It was a nice car, nice like your sister, nice like the girls your mother never understood why you didn't ask to the prom. The original Corvette with Blue Flame Six, side curtains, two-speed automatic and swoopy good looks fitted one market fairly well. It was a country club sports car, fine for the fellow who relished a

Pages preceding: 1953 Corvette • Owner: R. Conover / Below and right: 1954 Corvette • Owners: Mr. and Mrs. William R. Locke

1954 Corvette • Owner: M.L. Young

pleasant drive in the country. Fine, too, we snickered, for a woman. But we men . . . well, we bought a Jag, a new one if we could afford one, a used one if we could find one—or if neither of those avenues was open, we simply pined for one.

Brace yourself. There are two giant steps coming in short order.

The first was the Thunderbird Revolution. Ford had lagged a bit behind Chevrolet, in that Ford's entry for the driving pleasure market didn't arrive until 1955. The early 'Bird, the two-place model, was a stunner. Never had a car looked better parked by the golf course. Never had a pretty girl looked better behind a steering wheel. The Thunderbird had . . . style.

Kicked hell out of Corvette sales. More important in the long run, and the reason this writer believes it was a revolution, was that the Thunderbird didn't need to be driven. You just lolled back and steered.

Sports cars were in, most strongly with people who didn't know what a sports car was, either. Came the Thunderbird, with all that style and grace and with no demands upon the driver and socko! the front lots of Ford agencies up and down both coasts were jammed with second-hand M.G.'s, Triumphs, Jags, Healeys, Porsches.

Made us very happy. In my own case, what had been a hot rod club was transformed into a sports car club almost overnight. For the first time we could hand

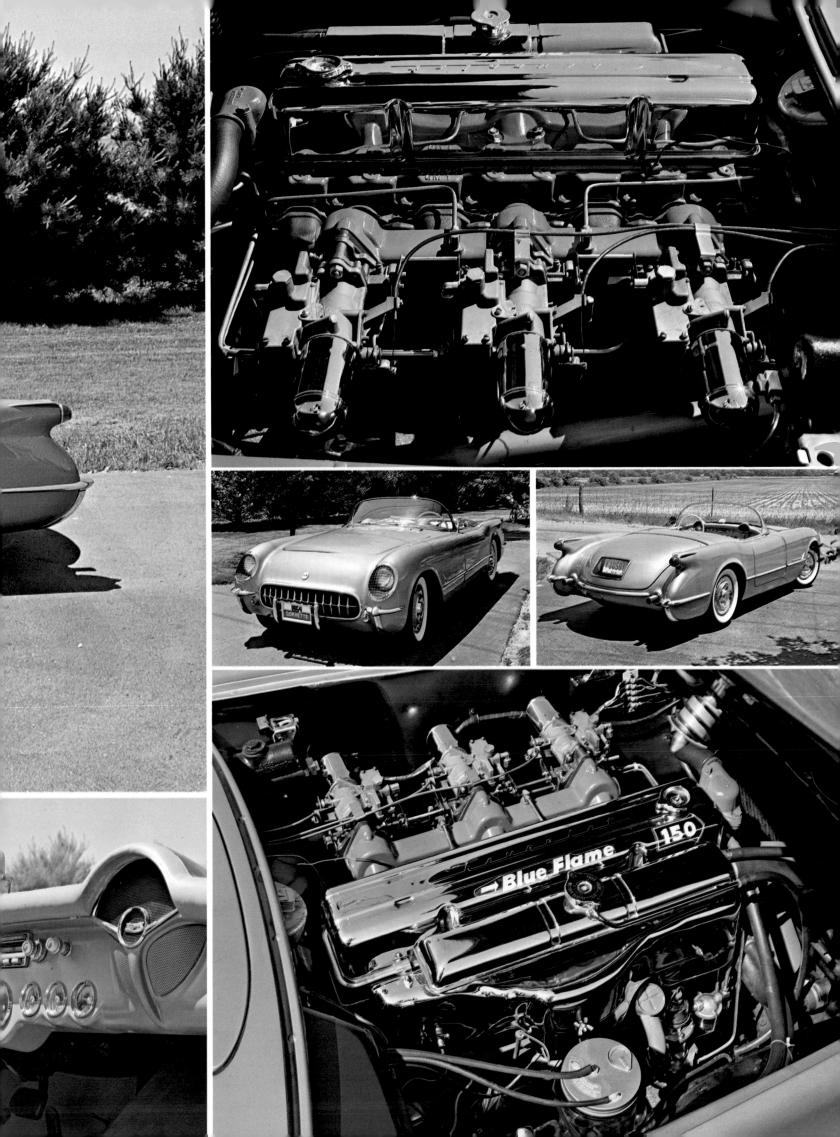

our A V-8's and '40 Merc convertibles with monkey-motion (overhead valves to the kids in the audience) V-8's on to the next generation and get that Jag we'd been hankering for. *We* knew that sports cars were to drive fast in, even if the effete country-clubbers and their bleached wives didn't.

The second step began with such logic as to have been nearly hum-drum. Shortly after World War II, the various car companies all blossomed forth with overhead valve V-8's. The postwar cars needed larger and more powerful engines to haul the larger cars and the overhead valves were more efficient than the old flathead eights and sixes, and the V configuration gave a stronger engine that took up less space.

All the makers wanted was stout and reliable passenger-car engines. Chrysler had the most stout and the most powerful, then came Cadillac, Oldsmobile, et al. Ford was nearly at the end of the line with its ohv V-8 for model year 1954. While it wasn't an especially good engine, it did give the Thunderbird enough poke for its market.

Recent histories of the Chevrolet engine have contained hints by the engineers responsible that when they were working away on the drawing boards, they sort of knew and worked toward the domestic V-8 as a racing powerplant. Hmmm. If so, and if they were prudent, they kept it quiet. Chief engineers aren't pleased to catch the young turks playing boy-racer on company time, and even if the chief is himself a closet speed nut, the board of directors expects to get what it orders, i.e. a reliable passenger-car engine with enough power, cheap to build, working life of 100,000 or so miles.

The Chevrolet V-8 was much more than that. It was smaller and lighter than the

other V-8's, to the point that the hot rodders of the day called it a "mouse motor," which shortly became a term of affection. The combustion chambers were right, the odd stamped steel rocker arms may have been put there to save cost, but they let the Chevy engine wind higher than the others. In short, the Chevrolet V-8 was right.

In exactly the wrong place. This wonderful new engine. We hardly noticed it at first. But I digress.

This is hard to credit now, more than twenty-five years later, but from 1932, the year of the Ford V-8, to 1955, the year of the Chevy V-8, the words Chevy and Performance simply didn't appear in the same sentence. In high school I knew a kid who liked Chevies. I also had a cousin who didn't like corn on the cob. I thought of them as equals. On a one-to-ten scale of normality, both would score two.

Then early in 1955, a few months before my club converted from street racing to road racing, a new car showed up at the venue where we conducted what the state vehicle code still quaintly terms "displays of speed." The owner was the son of the man who ran the body shop for the local Chevrolet agency. He had a two-door coupe, red and white with a black top Dad did (maybe?) on his own time. The newcomer had been practicing. He knew something we didn't know.

He blew our doors off.

Beat the Rocket 88's, the ohv Fords, even the Buick Century I drove in match races for a wealthy friend whose own license was in peril. Sure, the stock 265 Chevrolet was no match for my Winfield-Ford or the Olds-Mercs, but the '55 Chevy had two clean lengths on any stock car we could come up with. And we looked.

1955 Corvette • Owner: Leroy Whisman

There was more. The first Chevy V-8 had a two-barrel carburetor and single exhaust. They followed that with the Powerpack, a four-barrel carb and dual exhausts. If you got too involved and wound the engine past peak, the valves floated. The cure for that was the Duntov Cam, a name we whispered ten or fifteen years before we learned Duntov was a person. From then on, when Chevrolet spoke, we listened.

Chevrolet almost kicked this keen thing away. Until I began looking up all this detail, the 1955 Corvette was a blank. There were vague mentions in the magazines, the club stuff, but in the casual mind there was the original Corvette, '53-'54, and the rocket Corvette of 1956, and fuzzy space between, containing only references to the fact that Chevrolet didn't sell many Corvettes in 1955 and almost quit making the car entirely.

Image. The original pleasant, undemanding Corvette had been floating around the golf clubs and suburban railroad parking lots for two years when the V-8 went into production. Chevrolet offered the V-8 as a Corvette option. According to the records, a handful of buyers chose it. Nothing happened. The car looked the same, so the lack of appeal for the genuine car enthusiast remained the same, i.e. barely there at all.

However. Important decisions were being made at Chevrolet Division. Perhaps it was simply sound business judgment. Ford has the country club set, they said, we have in our employ men who can and have built true high performance cars. Let's go for the people Ford is giving away. Let's build a performance car.

Americans weren't buying sports cars because sports cars had side curtains. They

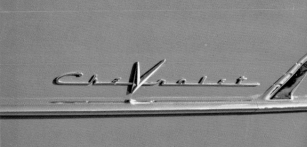

1955 Corvette • Owner: Pat Connell

Pages preceding: 1956 Corvette, owner modified • Owner: Larry Royston / Above: 1956 Corvette • Owner: Pat Conn

Below: 1956 Corvette • Owner: Tom Souza

didn't care if the headlights looked at home in a (shudder) rallye. Jaguar and M.G. tops did flap and leak. The doors flew open, the radiators lost their lunches and the fuel pumps sulked at the slightest hint of rain. No matter. No matter at all. It was what happened behind the wheel on the open road that mattered.

America is the land of wide open spaces. Chevrolet recognized that. Speed and power. If enthusiasts in other countries had small and intricate engines for tax reasons, if they could make do with power sufficient to pull a robin off its nest, that didn't mean the American sports car driver (or the American sports car) could get by with only enough power to break the speed laws. We needed power. Raw Power! Pushrod Power! And if we needed to know the right numbers for the right ear so we could get more power than the factory sold to just anybody, so much the better.

Most important, the power had to show, witness the slump of 1955. New wine in old bottles, the English say. The optional V-8 was a case of white lightning in a milk carton. (Yes, of course, the original Corvette was white.)

Another surprise turned up in research is that the 1956 Corvette was strongly based on the original. Somehow the impression was all-new car. Not so. The keener minds at Chevrolet Engineering went out and reworked the chassis so it would handle at the ragged edge. Same basic layout, but with revised roll centers and stiffnesses and so forth.

The body got the real work. Not one line remained the same. The pictures tell the story and this is not the place for art criticism. Suffice it that the eggcrate grille, the forward thrusting headlights, the tapered tail and the sculptured panels aft of the front wheel opening transformed the car. The result was breathtaking. The first body looked parked even in motion. The second style seemed not only to be at speed, but to be poised, crouched, coiled, ready to spring into even greater speed.

The timing was perfect. By model year 1956 Chevrolet had the greatest stockblock engine of all time. They had a coterie of guys who loved and understood performance cars planted deep in the home plant, and at work selling the car. They had a good chassis. They had that body. Surely no sports car ever looked more *right*, more in tune with its time, or perhaps more accurately the time that was now so fast approaching.

Finally, they had us, all the car nuts, the sports car enthusiasts who had just found out driving could be a good time, and driving on roads was better than stab and go straight. If all effective preaching is to the converted, it follows that a willing audience is as important as the message.

So. To say Chevrolet did it right is to leave out half the equation. Chevrolet supplied the material and . . .

We did it.

Fun, Frustration, Fuel Injection

For those of us wicked—and human—enough to relish the mighty being humbled, racing has always been great theatre. In the case of the Corvette, this goes double, as the marque has served as both humbler and humblee.

The first taste Corvette had of racing must have been more like a snack of crow. The original version was not supposed to be a racing car. It wasn't and the factory made no claims to the contrary. The image back then had a vague touch of effeminacy, what with the automatic transmission and the poor old Six.

When the Corvette got the fierce V-8 and then was given a body to match the engine, the Corvette grew what was known in those days as hair, which subsequent cultural evolution has rendered into the term macho. Corvette became a man's car, a young man's car and that meant racing.

In 1956 sports car racing was controlled by two generally shared and accepted illusions. Then as now, illusions were more powerful than truth and illusions had the authority equalled only by booming voices out of the sky.

The first myth was that all sports car racers were ordinary people who only wished to enjoy their sport. To do this, they drove perfectly stock cars to shop and office during the week and then drove to the track, where they removed spare tires, fiddled with the engines, raced and drove home, all for fun and little silver cups.

At one time, say the first sports car racing ever held in the United States, this might have been true for some racers. As a myth it did no harm. The harm came from the rules. Because all racers were presumed to be out for fun in stock cars, the rules required all cars to be stock.

Because the top drivers were in it for fun and fame and glory and girls, that is, they wanted to win, the normal reaction to purely stock rules was—if you were a private party—to cheat. Or—if you were a manufacturer planning on selling cars because they won races—to fit the competition cars with what were referred to as options.

44   That's a broad word, options. The domestic factories learned how to do this when stock sedan racing became popular and Detroit offered great lists of export suspension packages and high-altitude cylinder heads, both of which made the cars fast at Daytona, and few of which ever saw the border or the Rockies.

The sports car makers overseas had gone through much the same thing, but for sports cars. They had special cylinder heads, camshafts, big brakes, choices of final drive ratio, tiny windscreens, big fuel tanks, even aluminum bodies. As with Detroit, the pretense was that the ordinary customer could order his go-to-work car with all this racing gear attached; the fact was they made as many hot cams and triple-carb manifolds as they figured the factory team would need that season.

The second illusion was that all cars were designed and created equal. The classes for production and modified cars were based entirely on engine size. If you owned, for example, a car with a two-liter engine, you raced against all other production cars with two-liter engines.

The result of this was no more surprising than were all those options. The expensive cars had more power and less weight per displacement and the expensive cars won. Porsches beat M.G.'s—until in this case, M.G. owners having more votes than Porsche owners, the SCCA created a class break to keep the two marques apart—and AC-Bristols beat up Triumphs and so forth, up and down the displacement and price scale.

Well. At about the time people at Chevrolet decided they'd talk about racing, the engineers went out on the proving ground and ran a Corvette at high speeds, straight and around turns. At the car's limit—or what they thought was the limit, an important distinction—the car became something of a handful. So they beefed up here and there and pronounced the car ready.

They were about 10% wrong. The '56 Corvette in racing trim, as the factory believed, had a fine engine in the 265 with dual four-barrel carburetors. The three-speed transmission was adequate and the drum brakes were as good as the drum brakes used by just about everybody.

1957 Corvette • Owner: Ron Weidner

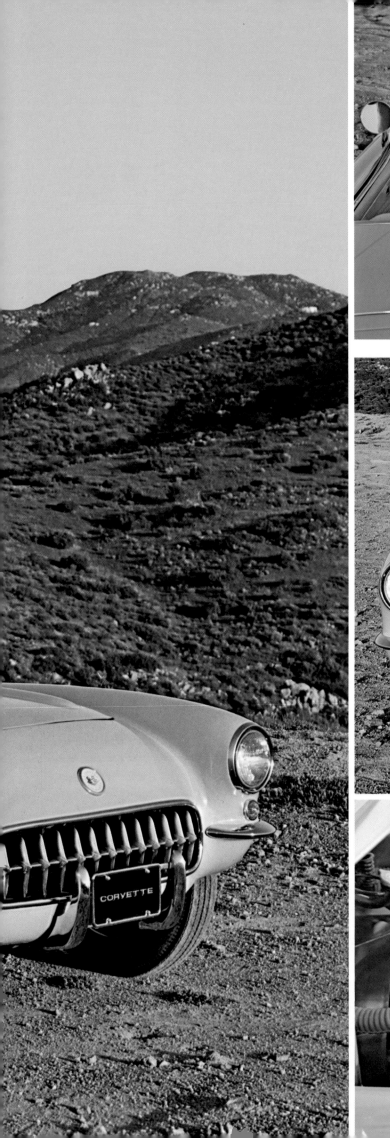

1957 Corvette • Owner: Wally McPherson

Corvettes didn't have maximum power and they didn't have the best handling. Corvette also had capable competition in the form especially of Mercedes-Benz. That fabled factory mauled the entire racing world in the early Fifties and the company followed with a road car that really did have engine and chassis improvements derived from racing. It was expensive as hell, it required trained professional care and it had a list of options from here to Stuttgart.

Some forms of racing can be conquered in the lab and some forms can't. The Corvette factory team—so to speak—built cars for top speed, went to Daytona and picked up all the prizes. Speed is easy. You figure how much power it'll take to set a record, you tune the engine until it puts out that much power and you go out and set the record.

Then there was Sebring. A funny race in a funny place. Sebring filled a void we didn't know existed until it was filled. Sebring was a cagy promoter who persuaded the people of a small Florida town to help him use their leftover airport for the benefit of their volunteer fire department. Sebring became an endurance race, the 12 Hours of Sebring. If it wasn't Le Mans or the Mille Miglia, it was at least a place we could go every spring and if we couldn't go, we could sit in the dorm and listen to long-playing records of wonderful cars speeding down the bumpy old runway.

This folk event became the most important road race in the country and the Corvette people decided to tackle it. Zora Arkus-Duntov, a road-racing engineer who did wonderful things on his own and then wandered into Chevrolet looking for things to do and was quickly hired as the perfect man for the job, rounded up a semi-pro team and they quickly assembled cars and options.

In the immediate sense, it wasn't enough. Long road races aren't won in the lab. The cars weren't fast enough or quick enough or strong enough. This became clear early on and the team straggled.

In the longer run, it put us fans on notice. Corvette was in racing. It gave the team people a much better look at what winning takes, so they could design and produce winning cars.

Two sidelights. One was that this type effort became something of a Corvette (or Chevrolet) weak point. For the next couple of years guys from the division or the factory or in disguise would show up with all manner of odd machine. They usually failed and they usually did that because they simply were too fancy; experimental brakes or the like which worked just great until . . . and there always was an until

Remember options? The Duntov cam mentioned earlier was one option. It was a new profile and it gave the 265 and later V-8's more power and more revs, without

Left: 1958 Corvette • Owner: Bob McDorman / Below: 1958 Corvette • Owner: Eric B. Robertson

Corvette goes Hot Rod, menacingly: at top—the '59 converted by Dennis Tracy to NHRA
Gas Car or Bracket Racer, the '62 of brothers Renfroe, 1976 G/Gas IHRA record holder.

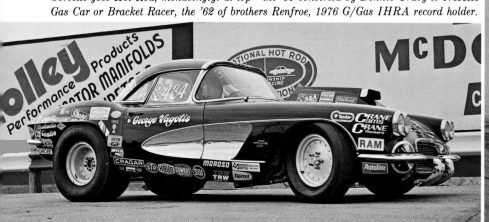

From the left: Corvettes competing in NHRA Springnationals at National Trails Raceway (Columbus, Ohio), 1977. Below: Winston Championship Points Meet, Indianapolis, 1977.

making the engine unsuitable for the street. Idle was just rough enough, too. Along with obvious things like that, when they built the Sebring cars they fitted them with oversize fuel tanks, cerametallic brake linings, limited-slip differentials, magnesium wheels, special shock absorbers—and all these delightful items found their way into public, one way or another. Odd. Nothing in the official literature says anything about this, but as this is being put to paper, the writer knows not only of a model known as the Sebring Replica, but of three such replica team cars now undergoing restoration. They are, as you'd guess, early Corvettes equipped with

every competition part known at the time. Keen car and any questions as to if such a model ever was produced for sale out of a showroom will be met with a reply like, You just wish you had one. Which I do.

Came then a glimmer of success. Two California hot rodders, who actually did work for *Hot Rod* magazine, name of Racer Brown and Bob D'Olivo, went to the sports car races and watched a Corvette get whipped. Didn't enjoy it. They wrote to Chevrolet and said they could do better than that and the next thing they knew, a Corvette had been placed at their disposal.

This was a delicate business. The car came

with electric top lift, radio et al., a sign of what Chevrolet knew about racing. It also had electric window lifts, which turned that table because the motors were lighter than the manual cranks.

Chevrolet has always been reserved about racing involvement. The car was actually owned by a dealership, the work was done in D'Olivo's garage and the expenses were paid by Chevy's ad agency.

The two backyard wrenches didn't care. Brown built better engines and D'Olivo went to the spring shop and picked out piles of new springs and anti-roll bars, beefy as possible. They took the car out for testing

Pages preceding: 1958 Corvette • Owner: Ruth Motors / Left: 1959 • Owners: Bill and Mary Ann Swanson / Below: 1960, owner modified • Owner: Marshall Kahn

and learned the problem was merely that the Chevy engineers had pushed the car to their proving-ground limit. The racing limit was an extension of that. West Coast sports car racing then was done on airport strips and in occasional parks, in towns where the racers were also the social and business leaders and had clout enough to close off the public grounds for a weekend or two. More power and stiffer suspension and a hot rod technique worked fine. The pioneers lined up Bill Pollack, who had been driving Allards and thus knew all about brute power and handling, for events put on by the California Sports Car Club. For SCCA races they relied on Dr. Dick Thompson, a Washington, D.C. dentist who'd been one of the top Jaguar drivers in the East.

Then they beat the fearsome Mercedes, head to head. Humblee to Humbler in less than one season.

To list Corvette victories since then would be to fill the rest of this book with tiny type. Suffice it that while the factory guys were winning some and overcomplicating others, that first win was followed by countless wins, as Corvette became a sports car which any good amateur mechanic, any brave and fairly skilled driver, could use for racing. Corvette turned the illusion about sporting types out to win for fun, on their own, into fact. Been doing it ever since.

While the Corvette was becoming a car for amateurs, the professionals had developments of their own. In the mid-1950's fuel injection became public knowledge—to use the cliché—with Mercedes-Benz. That firm brought f.i. into racing and then extended the system into its production cars. Mercedes used an elaborate and excellent fuel injection, as far as the principle could be taken at the time.

Also at that time, the four-barrel carburetor was fairly new and not completely understood. Getting the precise mixture control required for racing, under changing atmospheric conditions, was a bit beyond most tuners. And as cornering speeds and side loads increased, so did bothers with keeping the fuel level at the right place.

Chevy engineers ran feasibility studies and decided that while a complex system à la Mercedes would cost more than the gains would be worth, they could devise a simpler system, 90% of the power for maybe 20% of the money. And they could do that as easily

1960 Corvette • Owners: Mr. and Mrs. William R. Locke

Pages preceding: 1961 Corvette, owner modified • Owner: William D. Mullen / Above: 1961 Corvette • Owner: Bob McDorman

Above: 1961 Corvette • Owner: Ron Weidner / Below: 1961 Corvette • Owner: Phil Roche

Left: 1962 • Owner: Eric B. Robertson / Above: 1962 • Owner: W.H. Heinrich / Pages following: 1962, owner modified • Owner: H.D. Walterhouse

as they could work the bugs from the four-barrel carb. Another and—Chevrolet Motor Division would reap a giant gain in status, a benefit the men in charge of money could understand.

Fuel injection sounds frightening to those of us who sometimes can't figure out mechanical things we see every day. All f.i. actually means is that there's a pump pushing fuel into the airstream, rather than a bowl of fuel being pulled into the stream by the passing air. The Chevrolet system had a constant flow, with mixture controlled by sensing devices, throttle opening and such. (The Mercedes f.i. in its 300 SL had six tiny injectors, one for each cylinder.)

Actual development and selling the idea to management and working out the bugs proceeded well. For 1957 the Corvette had the same body and suspension, the V-8 was bored out to displace 283 cubic inches and with fuel injection the engine was rated at 283 bhp. One horsepower per cubic inch, as the factory was not reluctant to tell us.

(Worry about this. The author has in his possession a secret power chart, drawn up years ago by a spy/engineer. It uses a car's test weight, and speed through the timing lights at a certified drag strip, to come up with a good estimate of an engine's actual power. This chart indicates that *if* the testers were doing their best and *if* the scales and lights were accurate, then the 283/283 Corvette tested by *Road & Track* in 1957 didn't quite develop 283 bhp. The author's guess is that the dyno reading used for the rating and the ads was, shall we say, an optimum one, a reading which had all the luck and factors going for it?)

Along with the engine came a new transmission, with four forward speeds. Bit of a backyard job, in a way. The engineers put the new first gear where reverse had been in the three-speed gearbox and plunked reverse into a revised tailshaft housing. Backyard but effective.

Four speeds forward were not needed so much for the actual performance as for reputation. All the imports had 'em, so sports car fans insisted, never mind that most of the imports needed lots of gears because they didn't have much engine. Duntov later was quoted as saying the team could have gotten by with three speeds and f.i. power, or with four speeds and the old dual four-barrels. Instead, the team got both.

Plus. D'Olivo, the chassis man from 1956, was asked if the factory guys took all his

wizard work and ran. Goodness no, he said. They knew all the tricks. They just hadn't been able to feed them into the system as fast, big companies being slow. The '57 Corvette was offered with an option of stiffer front springs, stiffer rear springs, bigger shocks, larger anti-roll bar, quick steering, limited-slip differential with choice of three track-only final drive ratios, finned and scooped brake backing plates and cerametallic brake linings. All in one package, mind. Mark the order form with that, the fuel injection and the four-speed and all you needed to buy outside the dealership was stick-on numbers, a roll bar and a helmet.

Oh, and in 1957 the car factories got together and agreed not to support, encourage or take official part in racing. Chevrolet honored this in several ways, the best of which was to be sure every high performance part produced by the factory really was available to the general public.

A couple of years after this the SCCA changed from stock-with-options to no options and any modification you could come up with. Thanks mostly to the incredible array of racing parts from Chevrolet, Corvettes went right on winning.

Early Corvettes and late Fifties racing: Riverside, above

The market was changing as well.

No car can be much better than the people who build it or the people who buy it. Buick produced a big, flashy car in 1954 and the public loved it. Ford did the same in 1957 and took first place in sales. So Chevrolet built a big bulgy car for 1958 and took back the sales lead.

That era was not one which will become revered for good design. As the Chevrolet and rivals grew fins, spangles, four headlights and similar detrius, so it followed that even the Corvette, clean and muscular car it was, had to gain weight and geegaws as well. The 1958 and '59 were the same basic contour, made larger and with extra lights, false vents and such.

Didn't actually hurt the car, though. It might have even broadened the Corvette's appeal, although I hasten to say here that not all buyers or enthusiasts for this body style were persons lacking in taste.

Witness my dad.

My father was the least likely sports car

At Elkhart Lake in '58, above; and, below left, a harbinger of Corvettes to come, the Sting Ray in red at Elkhart in '59 and in gray for the '60 Times GP at Riverside.

fan of my experience. When he was a young sport, he had a big Chrysler. Then he got married and switched to a secondhand Ford, a new Plymouth and a series of Buicks, like any normal prosperous man of his time.

My older brother sold his channeled '32 Ford coupe just in time to buy an Austin Healey and go off to college. In those days—Lord, how long ago this seems!—proper men's colleges didn't allow freshmen to have cars. My brother left the Austin Healey in the garage, with instructions for my dad to run it every few weeks. Keep up the battery and so forth.

Well. Until this time, my dad was the sort of person who actually was puzzled because I bought an M.G. TC rather than a Willys Jeepster. Both cars looked the same to him, that is, damned odd and out of date, and the Jeepster could hold four people. Everybody knew a car had to have room for four. What if you wanted to take your friends along? (I told him my friends preferred to drive their own M.G.'s, which

was true and went right over his head.)

But he was always willing to help, so he began taking the Healey around the block. Then he took it downtown. The he took it downtown with the top down. He learned how to fold the windshield into the full-speed position. He bought a cap. My mother got a scarf, with little M.G.'s and Jaguars and Porsches all over it. I drove past a parent-type social event one night and chuckled mightily at the sight of countless station wagons and one Austin Healey, British racing green with the top down, parked all in a row. My dad, the pioneer.

Then my brother came home from college.

"I am buying a Corvette," my father said.

I scarcely dared ask: "Stick or automatic?"

"Four speed stick. That's what it's all about."

Red and white, too. I didn't get to drive it much but what comes to mind now is the roughness of it, the harsh ride, the heavy steering, clutch and shift . . . and the power.

Oh, didn't it go, especially when my M.G. was about as quick as most cars. Nail the long thin pedal in the Corvette and the rest of the world dropped into a dot in the mirror.

Also it was strong. Dad drove it until his bursitis forced him into a Mercedes 230 SL with automatic. He sold the Corvette to my younger brother, who drove it until his carelessness in re the rearview mirror had various law enforcement officials counting on him to support the court systems on half the Eastern Seaboard. He sold it to a friend and I expect it's out there somewhere, still rough and still fast.

As a defense for good taste, the 1960, '61 and '62 Corvette bodies became progressively cleaner. The public had caught on or become satiated or something. Besides, Bill Mitchell and Duntov and friends had been doing styling work and running a semi-race custom car and they had big changes in mind, which were hinted at with the looks of the '62 body. For '63, they had a revolution.

Comes the Revolution

My wife tells me I am wrong. Our middle son did admire Sam's car, she says, but in point of fact, his first words were not "Sting Ray." Like any other tyke, his first words were Momma or Da-Da or Goo.

Perhaps. What I remember, though, was my son John at the age of one year and a few months. He was standing transfixed in front of Sam's 1963 Corvette Sting Ray, white, a coupe with that silly split rear window. Patient Sam, a kind man, was working the light switch and the headlights flipped in and out, in and out.

John's eyes were big as saucers.

"Sting Ray," he said to himself each time the lights performed their magic cycle, "Sting Ray."

He wasn't the only one. His rapt admiration may have been beyond what most car fanciers would have displayed but the car itself did transfix nearly everybody who saw it, both for its style and technical appeal.

The car—both the model name and the configuration—had a strange beginning. Remember those race cars Chevy displayed, as it were? One was a fast roadster with the normal V-8 tweaked to about double normal power, later to be replaced by the big-block V-8 first introduced for NASCAR racing. There really wasn't all that much Corvette in the car, as it had its own frame and body and brakes, but the looks were those of a lighter, smaller and cleaner production car. Even this can be a bit confusing, as the car began as a new body on the Sebring practice car from 1957, then had a series of detail changes and such in body style, various experimental brakes, a series of fuel-injected small-block engines preceding the big engine. The car was a show car and a race car. It ran against the best of the large modified specials of the day and while it didn't win lots of big trophies, it did fairly well. Nobody ever had to apologize. When the big front-motor cars had run their course, the Sting Ray became a display car and Bill Mitchell's play car. The Sting Ray was his own personal property. Racing is an expensive hobby, so it sure was lucky Mitchell held a top post in the GM structure.

The Sting Ray looked clean and different, with a high beltline, flat top panels and strikingly curved front and rear lower sections sweeping up to the beltline. The rear treatment appeared on the last of the second-series production Corvettes in 1962. That and a neater front end cleaned up the car to the extent there are those who'll argue that '62 was the year of the change.

Not beneath the skin. Came 1963 and the Corvette became the Corvette Sting Ray, a name completely justified by the game. The Corvette had independent rear suspension which had been developed from the experimental CERV I. A more powerful and tractable engine. Four speed stick. The hypnotic effect of hidden headlights. Convertible and coupe, the latter having an extreme pointed rear window.

The new Corvette was even smaller and lighter than before, a reversal of the oldest habit in the automobile world.

Pushing that beyond the limits of credulity, the cockpit was clean and tasteful and roomy. Yes. More leg room, more arm room. You snuggled, semi-reclining, into a proper bucket seat, got the pedal-seat relationship just right . . . and adjusted the steering wheel.

So. That's what it felt like to die and go to Heaven.

There is a temptation at this point to say the Sting Ray Corvette attracted a whole new type of enthusiast. On reflection, that would be wrong. What the new car did was give rational reasons to people who until now had resisted the Corvette's visceral pull.

Listen. Sports car folks are terrible snobs. Maybe because of self-defense from 'way back when imported cars were considered—honest—un-American, sports car fanciers tend to favor whatever it is the domestic product doesn't have. While the Corvettes were drubbing all the fancy imports, there were people saying, Well, sure, but it has that terribly old-fashioned live axle. When the Corvette Sting Ray arrived with an independent rear suspension, a good one, a system that worked and gave more traction than the journalists of the time could put into words, when the front suspension was reworked and the entire package was, to repeat, smaller, trimmer,

1963 Sting Ray • Owner: W.H. Heinrich

Pages preceding: 1963 Sting Ray, owner modified • Owner: Paul Webb
These pages: 1963 Sting Ray • Mr. and Mrs. William Johnson

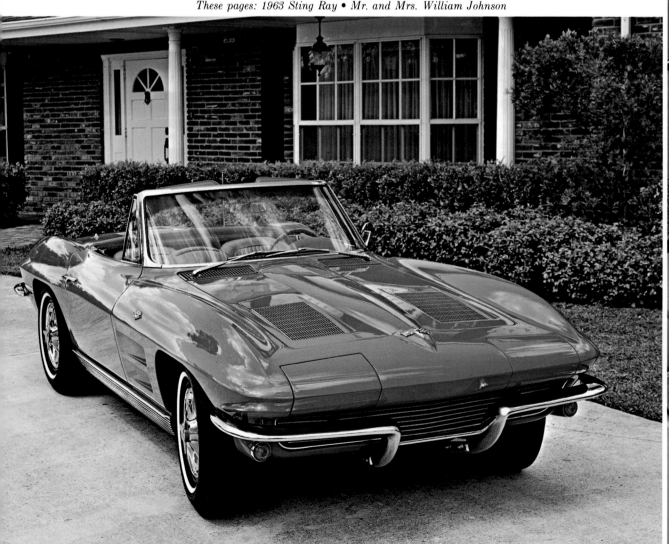

more comfortable and would also outhandle
the best of the bigger old Corvettes, why,
people who truly cared about technical
improvements bought Corvettes. (The others
decided it was disc brakes that counted.
We'll deal with that later.)

What happened in real life was the
Corvette racers, road and drag, were joined
by sports car people who simply enjoyed
driving, and sports car people who liked to
go on rallies and tours and like that.

Just as well. On the one hand, the
Corvette engineers truly had learned a lot
from competition and the Sting Ray handled
incomparably better than did the live axle
Corvettes. The Sting Ray had more
cornering power, more traction, rode better
and steered with more control. You went
faster with less effort. Even the competition
package was a giant leap beyond the older
competition package.

On the other hand, rules for production car
road racing were still odd. The poor SCCA,
as always, worked to please everybody and
pleased nobody. Chief threat was the Ford
Cobra, best of the true roadsters, last bastion
of brute force, as attractive as the Corvette
while weighing one-third less and selling for
half again as much. Corvette had numbers
and Cobra had power to weight. Cobra also
had a factory backing the team to the hilt,
solely to win. Corvette had a few bucks
filtered out and used for research. Because
SCCA wanted to keep all possible
involvement with the factories, and not to
allow a monopoly, the Cobra and various
Porsches and Ferraris were accepted as
production sports cars, never mind that only
a handful of the model in question was built.

Then SCCA did another strange thing.
Rather than use just plain engine size, the
SCCA divided the production classes into
performance classes. This meant that a jury
of experts picked, for example, the ten makes
and models which, if modified to the rather
loose limits of the rules, would be the fastest
ten cars around an average course. Then they
declared those ten models to be A
Production. The next group which roughly
averaged equal became B Production and so
on down the line.

There's a certain frontier logic to this. In
theory every owner could have a fair shot at
a win if he was willing to modify his car to
the limit. For sportsmen, this is better than
matching a 1300 cc M.G. against a 1300 cc
OSCA. At the top of the big production
classes, though, there were damned few
sportsmen. Oh all right, that isn't fair. At the
top every entrant was more than willing to
go the limit, nobody needed protection from
the big guy 'cause they all were big guys . . .
and the Cobra was the faster car around a
race track.

Corvettes won their share. Numbers did it.
There never were more than a handful of
Cobras racing at any one time, because there

1963 Sting Ray • Owner: Pat Connell
Pages following: 1963 Sting Ray, owner modified
Owners: Dale and Kathy Graham

weren't many Cobras built.

The Sting Ray sold in record numbers. The car can't be better than its buyers, remember, and the buyers knew a vastly improved car when it appeared. Kept the Corvette plant working two shifts, in fact.

The buyers competed. At the drags, in rallies and the real races. Sorry about the hint of sadness but the clearest memory now concerns a guy who literally was transported by delight in his car.

The SCCA allowed hill climbs, as sort of a speed event but not quite. You needed competition equipment but you could enter as a novice, meaning you could actually drive to the event in your stock and street-legal Corvette and compete with no license except a learner's permit, a novice license.

My chapter of the SCCA used to stage an annual hill climb on an abandoned highway outside a resort town in the Midwest. Lovely town. It lived on tourists and every year we got to drive from the hill climb course to the big old hotel in the middle of the town, with open exhausts, power slides through the turns, every trick we knew, while the citizens cheered and the police stood on the curbs, waving us on, Faster! Faster!

On this particular day I was at the finish line helping man the clocks when we heard the distinctive roar of a small-block Chevy V-8 and the equally distinctive whine of the four-speed Chevy transmission. Up the guy came, flashing around the curves, booming into the tiny straights, closer and closer, WHOOSH away, still under power past the finish line, still wide open.

At the timing station we stood looking at each other, too stunned to click the watches or lower the checkered flag . . . until there was the dull boomp of fiberglass hitting something solid.

We ran up. The driver was climbing out of a shredded Corvette. He wasn't hurt. Fiberglass is terribly good at absorbing impact.

Sorry, he said. I never had a chance to really open the Corvette up before and it all felt so right, I was so completely in tune with the road and the car and the speed and the sensations and all that, I didn't see the finish line, didn't know I was past it until the car was going so fast it slid right off the road.

Perfectly natural, we assured him. Could have happened to anybody.

Hypnotic is the word I'm after.

As the model continued for those first few Sting Ray years, it improved. One unquestioned step in that direction involved the split rear window. Classic conflict, in that Duntov didn't like the bar down the center and Mitchell literally would not allow the car to be built any other way.

Duntov the engineer wanted to look *out* and Mitchell the stylist wanted to look *at*.

Duntov bided his time. When the production cars were being built and Mitchell could drive one—he got so impatient at the time lag between the styling and being able

1964 Sting Ray • Owner: John Banner

to use his creations on the road he would have a show car built just so he could enjoy his own work before it was too familiar—so . . . when Mitchell finally got to sit behind the wheel and look at the rear view mirror filled with center bar, he growled, "That damn thing has got to go"—quoting Duntov fifteen years afterwards—and the '64 had a one-piece rear window.

The rear portion of the body was different. By the time they had more volume inside a smaller envelope and had put the spare tire and the fuel tank and so forth in the Corvette, there was no way to get a trunk lid, not without doing bad things to the looks or structural integrity.

So the Sting Ray and every Corvette since has had a spacious compartment behind the two seats and has provided not much access to the space.

Wasted? Not at all. My son John and his three-year-old brother and five-year-old sister would climb into Sam's '63 coupe the instant the door was opened. They'd scramble into a row and perch on the shelf just aft of the seats.

Sam would rev the engine, drop the clutch home and the Sting Ray would lunge into speed while the kids, giggling with glee, would roll into the pointed tail like so many pink-cheeked duck pins.

If "Sting Ray" wasn't John's first word, it should have been.

1964 Sting Ray, • Owner: Eric B. Robertson

The Sting Ray, Hairier Still

Research and hindsight make excellent bedfellows. Back when Corvette history was being made, it was made in the pages of magazines and all of us car nuts read every page, word for word, on lines and between them. During all this careful appreciation of the motorcar, we became somewhat skeptical: One sure way to prove you were a stone car fancier was to remark about how the factories turned out scores of incredible show vehicles while in the real world we got the same dull stuff.

Not so at all. Looking now at Corvettes back then, the same theme appears again and again: The best parts of the front-page flashers do come into production and it doesn't take long. The original Corvette went that route, so did the first Sting Ray . . .

. . . And so did the big block, known in the lexicon as the Rat Motor. (The small-block Chevy V-8 was the Mouse, so the big block, well, it really doesn't need explaining.)

Even with fuel injection and a modern suspension, the Sting Ray didn't win sports car races when matched against Ford's Cobra. The top men in the Corvette works didn't like this and they figured a way around the problem. Some form of word game enabled the men in charge to design a special Corvette, for racing only. They planned to have a short production run, 125 examples, and to sell the cars to various sportsmen who'd race them as GT cars and drub the other team.

The Gran Sport, as the project became known, was more like a replica Corvette than a racing model. Had its own frame and a special fiberglass body so thin you could nearly see through it. Girling provided some disc brakes, which were suitably modified. The body lines were cleaned up, that is, they removed the several odd decorations posing as vents and they replaced the fakes with real vents, scoops and like that. This was done in 1962 and there was no large Chevrolet V-8 so they worked out a special bored and stroked 327 that finally wound up at 377 cubic inches.

About the time the actual production was due to begin, the men in charge of the men in charge of Corvette got pressured by the men above them and issued an explicit set of rules. There was to be no factory racing. The old ban on competition was to be observed by General Motors and all its works. Ford could do what Ford pleased, Chevrolet was not to do anything like build a short run of racing GT cars.

The Gran Sport project was closed down in a blaze of glory. The actual five cars built, three coupes and two roadsters added to the program because they could be lower and thus faster on the straights, were sold to the Right People. The engines were swapped like mad, from the Duntov-modified 377 back to 360 bhp 327's and back to the 377 and later, in three cases, to the Rat 427. The Gran Sports did race and they did beat the Cobras fair and square on at least one occasion. Then the Gran Sports—which had after all gone to people who appreciated them—were retired and became road cars and collector cars. Haven't seen one for sale in years although you can bet the price is beyond rubies.

All this is by way of prelude. The 1964 Sting Ray had an optional f.i. engine with a rating of 375 bhp from 327 cubic inches. The 1965 news was real disc brakes. At all four corners. All Chevrolet. Seems the brake builders of the world had been invited to bid on Corvette disc brakes during the Sting Ray's gestation period but all said the car was too heavy for their products.

It wasn't that Americans didn't know how to build cars, it was that only Chevrolet was willing to build such a demanding system and it took a couple more years to do it.

The brakes destroyed the snobbish arguments about engineering, by the way. In the future the effete enthusiasts would merely sniff about Corvettes being so big. And with the brakes came a big engine. It began as a 396, reduced some from the original because GM wouldn't allow the smaller cars to have more than 400 cubic inches and it was the direct descendent of a Chevrolet engine which stunned NASCAR for a brief visit, that is, until GM yanked hard on the chain and got the wild racing guys back in their cages.

Bit of a brute, the 396. *Road & Track* was

Pages preceding: 1965 Sting Ray • Owner: Ed Wright / Above: 1966 Sting Ray • Owner: H.B. Shute

Below: 1965 Sting Ray • Owner: Don Magestic / Pages following: 1966 Sting Ray • Owner: Dr. Gerry Meier

Corvettes at the drags. Above: The F/G 1964 of Bruce Allen and Jim Hanley at the NHRA Springnationals, 1977. Above right: The H/G 1967 of Tony Christian.

At NHRA Winston Championship Points Meet, April 1977, two mid-Sixties F/G Corvettes. Below left: The car of Dick Weinle. Below right: The car of Bob Kamp.

Clockwise from above: The Competition Engineering 1964 D/Altered of Jerry Marquart; the '67 G/G "Checkmate" of Paul Mercure; the '63 H/G from Ault & James.

'63 split window in purple set up by Tracy Performance; the 1966 E/G car of Dave Hinton and Pete Scannell; the early Sting Ray H/G of Verguldi/Aloisia/Kelly.

A '63 split window coupe, stock body save for hood, with 305-cubic-inch Chevy engine, handcrafted dash, numerous other wonderments to behold • Owner: Dennis Trac

suitably impressed by the acceleration, best ever except for (what else?) the Cobra. But, said *R&T*, the car is heavier and the steering is too and so is the clutch and the gearchange and we don't think even this engine will get Corvette back into the winner's circle and anyway, while there are many sports cars which need more power, the Corvette surely isn't one of them.

That depends. *R&T* was wrong in a way. The SCCA performance-factored classes did (and do) work reasonably well when the racers are evenly matched for money and desire. The Corvette was allowed enough options to work well, having extra power to offset the extra weight. Also there was the power of numbers. Ford naturally countered with its big V-8 in the Cobra and there were some epic battles. In terms of wins-per-entrant I suppose the Cobra won the series,

so to speak, but all the fans cared about was the close racing, the battle of the brands.

The big-block Corvette involved more than racing. From the inside standpoint, it was a car Duntov never really wanted to build. During his tenure as resident enthusiast, Duntov always voted in favor of smaller, lighter, more agile and efficient. Sometimes he won, as with the early Sting Ray, and sometimes he lost. Not that he stayed in his tent and sulked. What really brought about the big V-8 was the rest of the world. Everybody had huge engines and Corvette had to go along with the trend. You can't build or sell a car too much better than the people who buy it.

A harsh remark. Perhaps not called for. What the big-block Corvette did was appeal to a new buyer, so it was a market expansion. This led to a division or

separation of sorts.

Has to do with image. When the thought first occurred, the break seemed along the lines of Realist versus Romantic. The small-block Corvette was lighter and strong for its size. The engine whizzed and wound, a banshee with pushrods which equalled the overhead cams of the imports. There was a certain pride of overcoming a handicap.

The big block simply meant the Corvette was mightier than anything on the normal road. None of this handicap stuff. Head to head, eyeball to eyeball, no quarter asked, no quarter given.

On reflection, while the above is true, both are still a matter of image. How often does one really get to open 'er up, to see wot she'll do? Leaving aside all the records and results and timed tests, the man with the small engine enjoyed knowing that he had a

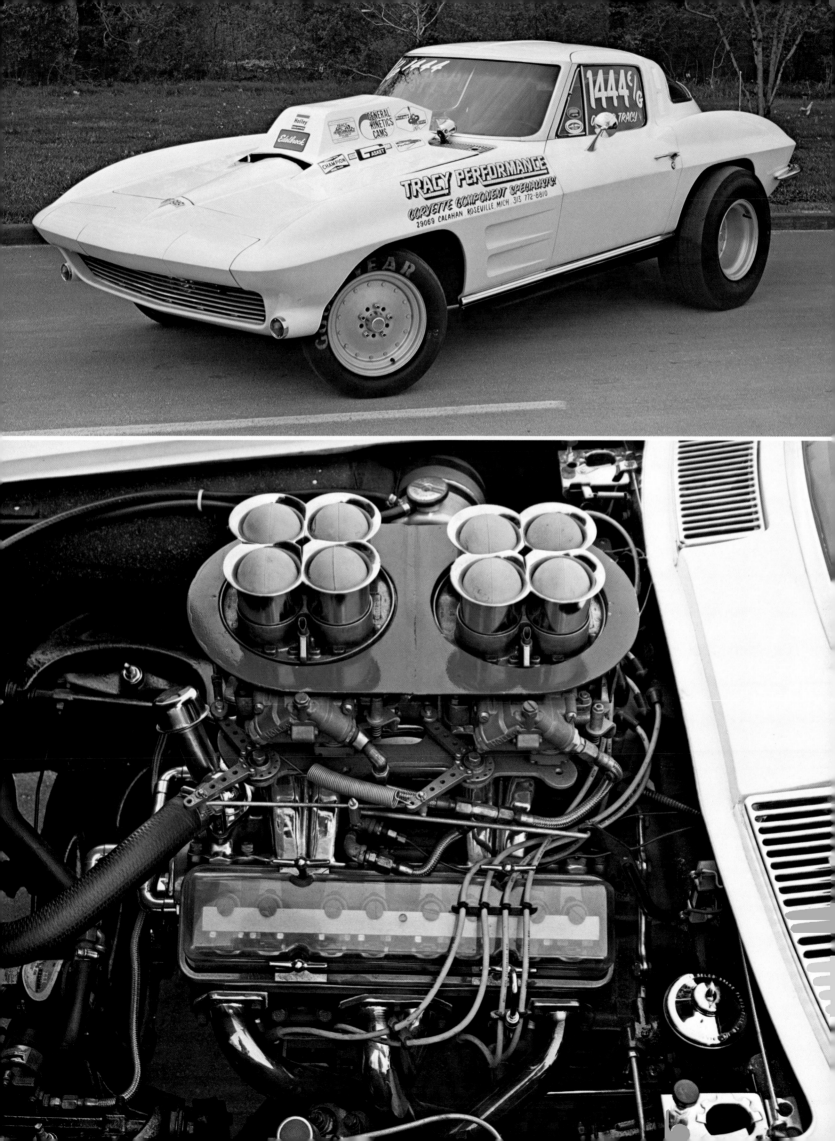

Above: 1967 Sting Ray • Owner: Gary Hoy / Below: 1967 Sting Ray • Owners: Terry and Shellie Tetzlaff

Pages following, Sting Rays from '67: Coupe • Owner: William D. Stephenson / Convertible • Owner: Tom Weber

Above: A '63 Sting Ray coupe, momentarily one trusts, pits at Bridgehampton. Above right: George Wintersteen's Grand Sport, also at Bridgehampton, 1966.

Below: The strikingly purple 427 Sting Ray of Mary Swindell leads a Lotus Elan and another Cor

wonderful engine up there, while the man with the big 'un knew nothing could stay with him if he chose to unleash the Rat's fury.

This was true worldwide. Our era's purest sportsman—a man whose name is withheld here because he's shy and besides about the time this book appears I will be driving one of his cars and thus am not willing to risk hurting any feelings—bought a 427 Corvette with the intent of competing in Europe.

The official factory charts don't show this but, according to my informed source, a year or so before the alloy-head, open-chamber, full-race 427 appeared as a catalogued option, it was a do-it-yourself option. Those who knew the right numbers could order a 427 Corvette with basic block and without the road version's extras. This model was legal for licensing, but it didn't actually run, not until you bolted together what amounted to an all-out NASCAR engine.

Above: Bob Johnson and his 427 in the Sports Car Club of America Regionals in October of 1966 at Mid-Ohio. Below: A Sting Ray takes on the Prancing Horse.

he SCCA National at Mid-Ohio, June 1966.

Off the owner went, to Europe. He entered all the classic road races there. Being a purist, he loaded the car with spares and actually drove on the roads to the road races.

He never got further than technical inspection. All his papers were in order, the car had been constructed according to the international rules but the soreheads in charge of the sporting venues did not see it that way. Each time there was some little thing which made the car unqualified for the race. Each time getting this little thing fixed took just enough time to leave the car in the inspection area until after the race began. And when he arrived at the next country and the next sporting contest, the fix he'd just done wasn't exactly what the new crew of officials wanted to see.

Right, this doesn't jibe with the experiences American factory teams had during this period. They did get to race . . . and they won. I suggest they had clout. I also tend to agree with this privateer's version of history because I was on my friend's team racing an English car in Italy a few years later and we were disqualified just as we worked into fourth place in a class containing ten Italian cars and us.

About the third time the Corvette wasn't allowed to race, the privateer reckoned there was a pattern emerging. Further, he couldn't see how it could be broken.

So he took his mega-horsepower Corvette with license plate onto the unlimited highways of Europe and cruised until confronted with various road-going Ferraris and such. Then—the car was pulling Le Mans gears and had a top speed of 170 mph or so—he raced the exotic cars into the ground. A few days of this and up stepped a European sportsman with cash in hand.

He knew what all those provincial officials knew. The 427 Corvette was the fastest car you could buy.

101

All for Corvette, Corvettes for All

Fortunate circumstances, or maybe a fortunate combination of same,'resulted in something of a peak Corvette Era in 1968-1970. One can—and this one reporter does—claim that this was the best Corvette, or best Corvettes, ever built. Personal judgment, of course.

The sheer impact of the car, the power and handling and racing record and style and nearly infinite number of combinations in which the car could be built, all those are beyond question.

The change from Sting Ray to Stingray, quoting from the identification badges on the cars, began as all Corvette changes seem to have begun, on Bill Mitchell's drawing board. About the time the show Sting Ray became the real thing, Mitchell once again drew up a show/styling car. This one was longer and lower and wider, with what can best be described as a Coke bottle profile, tapered between giant wheel wells, with an aggressive scoop for a nose and a racy flip at the tail. The hood was bulged and louvered and there were vents and scoops everywhere you looked. Not only that, they functioned.

Where all this came from I don't know. The tapered middle seems like something for supersonic airplanes, the flip tail surely was hatched at the same time the various racing works began fiddling with downforce. The front was probably pure Mitchell at his creative best.

In all, the styling was superb, the quintessence of what could be done. In one form, the Chevrolet people made a bold new statement, while at the same time the new shape remained Corvette and nothing else.

All right, the purists could carp. The new car was larger on the outside and—or so my measurements from the time indicate—was a bit more crowded on the inside. Still no trunk lid, still at least 3200 pounds in road trim, to carry two people. The wheel wells were seven or eight inches higher than they needed to be for actual clearance of the

wheels, all of which could lead to the conclusion that the stylists, maligned as always, had beat up the engineers and made function defer to form.

Untrue. Duntov had some corporate political hassles during this period, or so I read, he said nothing to me. But he and his staff took advantage of the new body to revise the chassis and suspension, once more in the interest of improved handling.

Fuel injection had been dropped two years before, as the carb people learned 1) how to make the four-barrel carb work in any racing or road situation and 2) that the public was willing to buy power even if it didn't have a fancy name.

What they did instead was work up a complete line of small-block V-8's, mild to wild, and a complete line of big-block V-8's, also mild to wild except that naturally the biggies were heavier and had more power. There was an overlap; the hottest 350's were hotter than the coolest 427's.

Behind all these engines went (on paper only, as we'll see) a three-speed manual transmission, or a three-speed automatic, or a four-speed stick with close ratios, or a four-speed stick with wide ratios. Behind them came a pick of gearsets, 2.3:1 to 4.11:1, if memory serves.

Coming out of another door, so to speak, were real racing engines, alloy-block 427's and alloy cylinder heads for the normal iron blocks. The announced intention was to provide something for the sporting racer, in production sports car and GT competition. The blocks actually saw more track time in the Can-Am cars of the day, notably McLaren. While the press of the era usually met the same guys coming out of the doors of both McLaren and Chevrolet, there's no hard proof that the Corvette option was a handy—well—loophole, although obviously that's just what I suspect.

So. Along with this bewildering array of mechanical marvels was a selection, yes, a

Right: 1968 Stingray • Owners: Evelyn and Norbert Jackson
Pages following; 1968 Stingray • Owners: Diana and Horacio Yates

Corvettes in performance during the 1968 season. Above: Learning a few things about competing, at St. Jovite, with the Montreal Motor Racing Club Driving School.

Below: Getting ready to start, Jerry Thompson buckling up prior to the send-off at Mid-Ohio Nationals.

selection, of body styles. There was the basic convertible, then a convertible with hardtop option, then a coupe.

Keep holding your breath. The circumstance cannot be described as fortunate, but during the Stingray planning, Congress (cries of "Fools!", "Knaves!", "Dupes!") passed laws declaring cars to be guilty until certified innocent. The bulk of the burden fell on low-production cars and Ford (repeat earlier cries) demonstrated it was only in sports cars for the money, by dropping the Cobra.

Bad for car nuts, handy for Chevrolet racing, ummm, racers. The Corvette became the only true production sports car made in America and because the United States made all the really hot performers, Corvette got an unbreakable hold on the top classes in production road racing. Oh, a private Cobra could show up and give the plastic jobs a run for the trophies, but that meant a lot of money going out and none coming in, so within a few years all the Cobras had been gathered up by collectors and used for club events, against each other and no other makes invited, or for driving around in public to frighten people.

The incredible choice of models and equipment made buying a Corvette something of a challenge. This was mass merchandising's finest hour. The factories had the option lists and production lines honed to perfection. They had been making the same bits for several years in large numbers and once they had the system working, with the combinations of engine/transmission/final drive/body style all arriving at the correct place at the correct time, having forty models was no worse than having four.

(It may not have been much better, either, as we'll see shortly.)

Whatever, we in the motoring press used to compete with each other and with our previous performances on an annual basis; what shall we do with the Corvette this year?

In 1969 the magazine at which I worked scored a substantial coup. We tested all the basic Corvettes, eight in total, including one and maybe two which the factory, for practical purposes, had on paper but not on the showroom floor.

To explain. When the '69 catalogue came out, there were three small-block Corvettes, with 300, 350 and 370 bhp ratings. The engines were mostly the same except that they had increasingly higher compression ratios, hotter cams and in the last example, better heads and carb. Then there were five big blocks, the 427 done the same ways, in short steps. Above the hottest of them was listed the alloy-block ZL-1, which was supposed to be a production engine except it never appeared for public sale 'cause the racers got all the hardware.

At the other end of the horsepower and performance race, the base Corvette for 1969 was supposed to have a three-speed stick

Pages preceding: The Umberto Maglioli/Henri Greder Corvette at Le Mans, 1968.   Tom Dutton, competing in B-Production and driving out of Bridgehampton

cho Valley in an SCCA regional during USRRC week-end, 1968.   Above: A '62 Corvette waltzing at the Englishtown NHRA Springnationals, 1968.

Tony DeLorenzo, son of a General Motors' vice-president, and Jerry Thompson, a Chevrolet engineer, were becoming rather formidable Corvette racers during 1968.

transmission. This was a marketing fiction. The four-speed mystique had conquered the world well before this. No self-respecting person would buy a three-speed. Well, some would maybe. In that year there were 300—and I probably should put quotation marks around the term—base Corvettes built.

Where they went was to dealers. See, dealers love to advertise bargains and a few clever ones would order the baseline 'Vette so they could claim lowest prices. Then the prospect would find out why the price was low and would allow himself to be talked into moving up one notch, to the mild V-8 with

four-speed, which therefore was actually the baseline car.

Not knowing this, we ordered a three-speed for test and were told there were none on the test fleet books, none in the fleet anywhere in the world and none would be ordered. If they built one for us, what would they do with it after the test?

Then came the hot little engine, the 350/370 LT-1. This was the stroked version of the 302 Z-28 motor then cleaning up in the Trans-Am series for Camaro. (The following year it became the 350 Z-28 motor.) The LT-1 didn't arrive because the Z-28 was selling so fast they didn't have all the hardware to

build Corvette engines too. Shows you where Chevrolet placed its priorities.

We worked around both problems, or rather, Chevrolet's sales computer and Corvette owners worked around them with us. They turned up a nice guy in San Diego who hadn't been turned off by three on the tree. He drove the dealer's come-on and liked it. He bought it. Made the dealer mad as hell, as he had to change all his ads.

A different kind of dealer had an LT-1, built for a customer. The shop had all the good parts, the cam and heads and carb, so they assembled the first 1969 LT-1 and sold it to the man who'd ordered it. The car was

Here they are shown, with DeLorenzo leading, at the Sports Car Club of America Nationals at Mid-Ohio.

covered under warranty, even, because it was all stock according to the books.

Heh heh heh.

Duntov himself showed up with a trucked ZL-1, which meant that end of the range was taken care of.

The test was a great success. More about that later. Lord, I forgot to say earlier that the surest bet in the motoring press business was a Corvette on the cover. Any time sales slumped or the issue-to-be had nothing much in it, we always used to figure some excuse for having a Corvette inside, and that meant a Corvette cover and the issue was bound to sell well. Never failed, nor has it yet.

Anyway, as noted earlier, the '68-'70 Corvette was in my opinion the best one yet. They all had marvelous brakes and handling, they all sounded fine without being overly loud, the handling was simply several years better than anything else domestic and as good as all but maybe two of the imports under all conditions.

They were all fast, which brings an odd reflection. First, they were on average much faster than anything being sold new at this writing. Even if you omitted the ZL-1, which would be fair seeing as how a twelve-second quarter mile with two people aboard dazzles but doesn't count because the car was not legal for sale to the public, the Corvettes were much quicker than modern cars with their low compression engines and inefficient tuning. Emissions, y'know.

Now the odd part.

They weren't that much different from each other.

Without going into all the figures and specs, the engines followed mostly a straight line except at the top. The racing version of the 427 had to have one four-barrel carb, due to rules. The top of the street-intended line, the iron 427, could have three two-barrel carbs, which meant more power. Further, that particular car had been built with quick test times in mind, and thus was possessed of a numerically high final drive and the close-ratio four-speed. The L-88 in the group was geared for top speed.

Here's the quarter-mile chart, elapsed times and trap speeds, for the:

300/350	16.12 at 84.46
350/350	14.55 at 97.93
350/370	14.44 at 99.90
427/390	15.02 at 93.45
427/400	14.70 at 97.60
427/435	13.94 at 105.63
427/430 (L-88)	14.10 at 106.89

Surprising, eh? Whip out and buy a copy of a current car magazine and check the figures. See how many, if any, modern sports cars can beat the time for the old lady's Corvette. Then turn the surprise around and wonder why the cars are so close. How much work and time and money, how much temperament and tuning, did we all accept as the penalty for cutting two seconds off our dragstrip times?

The same thing applies to the group test. The three-speed car was new and the owner wasn't a racer. In fact, he was a policeman. We didn't borrow his car for the track sessions, instead we drove it around town and country for a day. Very nice car, too. He was right. The Corvette in any trim had plenty of power and low-end torque. There was no reason for having a four-speed stick, except that they're fun to play with.

We did take the LT-1 to the drags. The owner was a slalom racer and was as anxious as we were to see how quick the car was.

Mighty quick. There was a substitute for cubic inches after all, and the LT-1 was it. In sum, the mild 427 was more like the mild 350 and the high performance 350 was more like the full race-designed motors than the displacements and power ratings (a joke, by the way; the low-rated engines had less, and the high ratings more, than the factory wished to reveal) would lead one to believe.

Nor did it much matter. Then as now, pretty near the only car capable of beating a Corvette, assuming the Corvette driver was one who cared about such things and thus would have taken the trouble to get the engine/drivetrain/etc. combination just right for him, was . . . another Corvette. If you're gonna lose, best it happens at the hands of someone with as much good taste and appreciation as yourself.

The L-88 Express, from L.A. to Phoenix

It was the best of days, it was the worst of days, it was damned near the last thing I ever did.

It was 1969. I was on the staff of that car magazine, now of sainted memory alas, and the reader will remember that we the staff had determined to do the Grandest, Most Complete, All-Encompassing Corvette Test of all time: each model in the catalogue put through the test procedure, topped by a visit to the GM proving ground and a talk with Zora Duntov.

After we rounded up all the models, a snag developed, namely that we could not use the proving ground. What we could do would be talk with Duntov and run the cars around a race track. Duntov and the track were in Phoenix and we were in California.

It was also the year of the Great Rain. All winter it rained and it was raining on the day we were supposed to drive three of the cars from L.A. to Phoenix.

The editor was a canny man. We had an LT-1, hottest version of the small V-8. We had the biggest selling Corvette, a 350 V-8 with 300 brake horsepower, automatic transmission and air conditioning. We had an L-88, the full-race production car.

Unless you looked real close, Chevrolet wasn't in racing then. Instead, Chevrolet was in the racing parts business. If you wanted to compete in SCCA production car racing, you could order a Corvette with the big motor, stiff suspension, giant brakes. This car had the extra-duty four-speed transmission known as the "Rock-Crusher." It had side exhausts and headers. It had, in short, every competition option known. It didn't have radio or interior padding. It did have wipers and defrosters and heater but that was because federal law didn't allow a car to be sold unless it had such fripperies and unless it was a road-legal car Chevrolet couldn't sell it.

This particular example also had racing tires. Big ones. For dry weather only.

It was raining.

Enter the thoughtful editor. He had himself, a sensible road driver; yours truly, a licensed racing driver who was smooth, sure and slow; and the tech ed, a licensed racing driver, record holder and demon tuner who knew the meaning of the word fear. He'd heard other people talk about fear but not having firsthand experience with that emotion, he looked it up in the dictionary.

"If we put — (he shall remain nameless) in the L-88, we'll never see him alive again," said the editor. "Same with me but for different reasons. I will take the sporting small-block, we'll put — in the road cruiser and you get The Beast."

The normal roads were washing out. We drove north into the mountains and had breakfast. Pouring rain. Mudslides. We didn't wish to worry about each other so we agreed not to convoy. We'd meet for lunch on the other side of the mountains.

The first hour was merely terrifying. The monster skated on those slick roads and treadless tires like, well, proverbs fail me. I didn't go more than fifty feet with the steering wheel steady. Mudslides blocked the road and I had to sit, chuffa, chuffa, rumble, while the 'dozers pushed a path through the rubble.

Over the crest and down, a roller coaster all the way but I was clear of traffic and if the L-88 got a bit far across the road on the tighter places, no matter. There was no traffic coming the other way.

Around a blind corner and . . . a flood. Water and mud blocked the road and on the other side of the stream there were twenty or so cars. Parked. I was doing about sixty, with maybe a hundred feet to the water.

I cannot say my life flashed before my eyes. More like a brief review of my misdeeds, namely the impulse that had me going too fast in the wrong place in exactly the wrong car and time. All these years as a motoring journalist, the big time, never a

1969 Stingray • Owner: Dick Schafer

Above and below: 1969 Stingray custom, "Mr. T's T Top" • Owner: Bob Titus / Right: 1969 Stingray • Owner: Carole Camp

Above: 1970 Stingray • Owner Craig Maxwell

Below: 1970 Stingray • Owner: Gene Holtrey

scratch on a test car. The only good part about crashing Zora Duntov's personal road-racing car was that I would not be around to explain it.

Wheels locked, I slid into the mud. A great brown wave sloshed over the windshield. I moved forward into the lap and shoulder belts, cradled my head in my arms on the steering wheel.

Nothing happened. The Corvette stopped. I turned on the wipers and the mud scraped away and through the smear I saw all the stopped cars, driving away. The guy with the flag motioned me to do likewise. Which I did, hoping, of course, to give the impression of a driver who gets through stuff like that every day.

Probably because after that things could only get better, things got better. The skies cleared and the temperatures rose as I got inland. We met for lunch (I said nothing) and after lunch I put down the top.

Oh glorious day. We cruised as fast as we dared through the clear desert air, chasing each other 'round the twisty bits in a sporting manner with—oh, all right—a touch of malice, as the quickest driver was in the slowest car.

Somewhere in Arizona, where the traffic was sparse and the road wide open and flat, one of the Interstates with the ten-mile visibility you get only on roads like that, something came over me.

My real self, maybe.

Here I was in a 500 horsepower car with license plates, a car geared and engineered for incredible top speeds for hours on end, twenty-four hours to be exact, and I wasn't using the car.

I did so. Foot down and the great gulping four-barrel gave its throaty roar and the needles moved in their circle until the tach and speedo told me I was doing an indicated 160 mph, probably an honest 150 but still a quantum jump beyond any speed I've ever experienced on the road or the track.

It felt perfectly normal. This truly was what the L-88 was born and bred to do. I sat there, slumped back in the reclined position mandatory in the second-generation Stingray, with the wheel firmly gripped at 10-2. The engine was right on torque peak and the pipes sang the clean, flat sound of a racing engine in fine tune, going about its appointed task. The rough ride became firm as the sign poles turned into a blur.

Beautiful.

How long this went on, I don't know. Speed in the L-88 was the perfect state, what the Zen crowd meant when they introduced the term With It. I was with the car, part of the car, not conscious of the car. Everything in me was lasered down to one unconscious flow, me and the Corvette.

At some point—half an hour, an hour, I don't know—conscious thought returned, in the shape of the sure knowledge that one cannot go this way at this rate in any state

on any highway for long. They have airplanes for people like me.

So I lifted off and eased back down to normal scofflaw, then pulled into a roadside rest and shut off the engine. I sat there, listening to the birds, the wind and the soft tick-tick of the cooling headers, until the other guys drove past.

We cruised into Phoenix. At the city limits, the L-88 transformed from coach to pumpkin. The tires nibbled at dots and stripes on the road, the clutch got heavier and heavier. Great waves of heat and fumes rose from the hood scoop and I growled from light to light, stop and go and stop and go. Oil pressure sagged and water temp rose and my shifting hand threatened to blister.

Duntov turned out to be a rare individual. Articulate, enthusiastic, good copy, as we say in the trade. We asked all the questions the press is supposed to ask and he answered, so we asked all the questions we weren't supposed to ask and he answered them too, while the p.r. man from Chevy wrung his hands and muttered about how all this was off the record, you guys wouldn't quote Zora on that, would you?—and of course we planned to and did, for the most part. The only bits we left out were those that could have hurt the man or the car.

Strange coincidence. Duntov has always been a nut about cars and Corvette in particular and one of the few non-technical regrets he had at the time was the people

who bought the models they bought.

There were, if memory serves, something like seven basic Corvettes in 1969. They ranged from pussycat small-block V-8 with hydraulic lifters and automatic transmission on up through powerful little engines and mild big engines to the L-88, an engine and a half, as described.

There was then a particular type of buyer (not limited to Corvettes, by the way) who figured value on the basis of price. The man—always a man—would walk into the showroom and order the most expensive Corvette in the catalogue. Well shoot, that's how it worked when he bought Cadillacs, why shouldn't it work with Corvettes? Of course it didn't work at all. Unless the dealer could dissuade him, and it's a rare dealer who sells a $5000 car when he can sell a $10,000 car, the case of too-much-money-in-the-wrong-hands got himself an L-88, five hundred great whacking wild horses and not so much as a radio.

These guys always seemed to live in metropolitan areas, or at least the ones who complained did. They'd write to Chevrolet and the letters would be transferred from headquarters to Corvette Central to Duntov's desk and he'd have the job of telling the customer just what a fool he'd made of himself.

"The L-88 is for the open road," Duntov said.

"Sure is," I said.

Above and below: 1970 Stingray custom • Owner: David C. Duggan
Pages following: 1970 Stingray • Owners: Keith and Judy Brown

Spell It With a "C" –Please

Only the name is wrong. Slip up behind the average car enthusiast, whisper "customizing" in his ear and he'll probably blurt out a reflex reaction of dismay:

"Customizing is metalflake paint and extended fenders and tinted glass and bizarre old Fords parked with one side jacked into the air so you can see the chrome-plated transmission housing. It's that funny fuzzy stuff they used to call Unborn Angel Hair strewn beneath the car. It's vans with mirrored ceilings and nice people like us don't do it. We don't even talk about it in public."

Yes and no. The word works against it. It has a kinky connotation, shared in this case by myself. Customized Corvettes?! I asked the editors, oh, come now.

Looking at the record shows there's a difference between what the word means now and what actually happened with Corvettes and the art, yes, art, of customizing.

Go 'way back. About the time the Model T Ford became everyman's car, every man started adding things and subtracting things to and from his Model T because he didn't want a car like everybody else's. Who does?

This was an add-on sort of business for the masses and a custom body business—every inch a business, too—for the upper crust, until after World War II. A few people began making really major changes to mass-produced cars and the techniques became skills shared by a handful and appreciated by, well, most every car fan of a certain age.

There became schools, or maybe directions. Two of them. You could take the original designer's statement and carry it further by two giant steps, or you could take the original statement and reverse it, for shock value and entertainment. (This latter direction was sort of a minor one, for very good reason.)

Consider school the first. Think about the '49-'50 Mercury, now known as the James Dean model. It was the first envelope body Mercury, with fenders flowed into the general body lines. It was low and sleek and had lots of gentle curves.

The custom people carried this to its extreme. The top was lowered by removing a few inches. The body was dropped on the chassis. The rear wheels were enclosed. All handles and knobs and trim were removed. The edges of the trunk lid and hood were rounded off and the lights were coyly tucked behind leaded rims. In short, the car was lower and smoother and sleeker and had more curves.

Reverse that. Think of a terrible example. Picture the poor little Nash Metropolitan, a rounded rectangle sitting on four little wheels and topped by a box.

Apply school one. Raise the body, make the wheels smaller and tuck them toward the center of the car. Raise the roof.

Awful. The custom Merc was attractive in its own way. A customized Metro would have suffered a fate worse than death.

The exception was racing. When you accentuate the positive, when you have a great looming supercharger sticking out of the hood of an Austin A40 or a 1939 Willys coupe wearing bulging drag slicks, you create a barely-controlled monster, which is just what the drag racing fans pay their money to see.

Well. What we have at this point is a technique by which a car can be different, and a technique which takes the starting point, in the appearance sense only, and takes it as far as the redesigner wishes to go. If you take the right beginning and go in the right direction, customizing works.

And now, respectability. Another popular journalist trick is to gather up a panel of freelance designers and ask them to redo the Corvette.

They love it. They've been waiting for this chance ever since graduation from the Art Center or the Rhode Island School of Design. Nothing they'd rather do than take up where the production men made Bill Mitchell leave off.

He started right. When you're in the big leagues, you don't build custom cars. You build show cars, and ever since the name Corvette appeared, all the regular line has been heralded by show cars, display cars, styling exercises or whatever name is being used at the time.

Corvettes begin as bigger than life. No,

1974 Custom Coupe, "Draggon Wagon" • *Owner: Jerry Pennington*

Below, above, right: 1964 Custom Roadster • Owner: Kevin Dennis / Page opposite center and below: 1965 Custom Coupe • Owner: David W. Mielke

really. Picture a VW Beetle flogging down the highway. The driver has his foot nailed to the floor, he's hunched over the wheel as his eyes swing back and forth, always worried about another threat, another lumbering something trying to get past. Mobile paranoia.

Here comes a '70 Corvette, a coupe with those flying buttress panels aft of the doors and the little flat rear window. The fenders bulge and yet they can't quite contain the fat tires. Blum blum blum blum, it glides by with that jiggly motion common to all high performance cars. All you can see is little heads. The people are too small! But it doesn't matter. They are in a magic carpet, a flying machine.

The Corvette, especially the Corvette since the Sting Ray, makes a statement. Shouts the statement. Trumpets power and speed and yes, excess. Here is a car that's too big for two people and my goodness, aren't they having fun!

We'll have to call it customizing because no other word really fits, but when we look beyond the prejudice, the pictures herewith are impressive. As works of art, which many of them are, restyled Corvettes please and excite the eye.

Contradiction in terms. Soon as we think about redesign, obviously we're talking of one man's view, or maybe a few men working together. Individual work. At the same time, we tend to group these individual expressions into classes or categories.

Time plays a major part here. Begin with the early examples and the changes are mostly to highlight what's already there: lower bodies, wilder lights, exotic paint.

Page opposite and below: 1965 Custom Roadster • Owner: Eugene Griman

Above: 1965 Custom Coupe • Owner: Richard Weinle / Below: 1965 Custom Coupe, "Froggy" • Owners: Carole and George Nix

Above: 1976 Custom Racing Coupe • Owners: R.L. Voit, Jr. and R.M. Proffit / 1966 Custom Racing Roadster • Owner: Skip DeAscentis

Two BB/FC Dragster Corvettes. Above • Owner: Don Gerardot / Page opposite • Owner: J. Jackson

Page opposite, below: 1966 Custom Racing Roadster • Owner: Charles W. Vandall / Below: 1974 Custom Racing Roadster • Owner: Rick Hay

Above: 1964 Custom Roadster, "The Dam" • Owner: R.D. Conners / Below: 1966 Custom Coupe • Owner: Ralph H. Eckler

Above and below: 1966 Custom Coupe, Mako Shark image • Owners: Tony and Cec Reed

Above: 1966 Custom Coupe • Owner: Mark Pierson

Below: 1966 Custom Coupe • Owner: Ron Russell

Custom Coupes. Pages preceding: 1966, "King Rat" • Owner: Keith Ball
Above and page opposite: 1968 • Owner: Jerry Pennington / Below: 1968 • Owner: Terry Holston

Above and below: 1969 Custom Coupe

"Super Vette" • Owner: David Hensch

Above: 1969 Custom Roadster, "Rabbitts Rat" • Owner: Tom Easterday / Below: 1968 Custom Racing Roadster • Owner: Richard Weinle

Above: 1968 Custom Coupe, "Yellow Tail" • Owner: John F. Firth-Smith / Below: 1969 Custom Coupe, Mako Shark image • Owner: Glenn Lehman

Above and below: 1969 Custom Coupe • Owners: Tom and Char Whitlatch
Page opposite: 1969 Custom Coupe • Owner: John R. Palinkas, Jr.

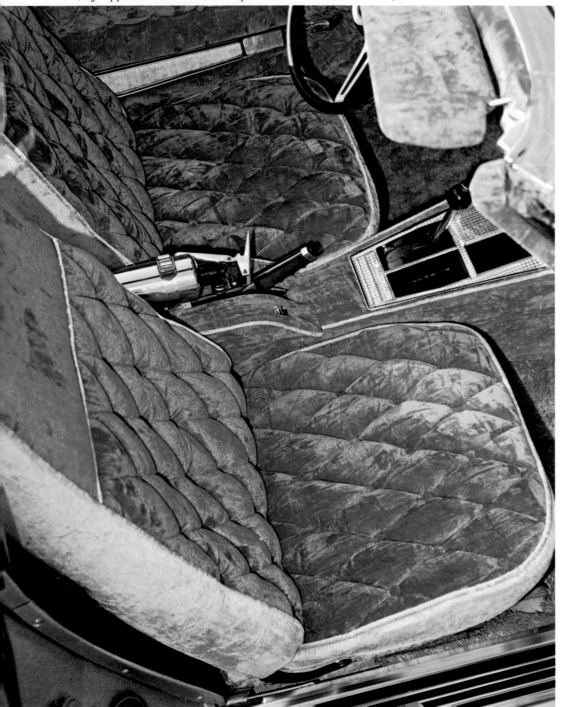

Minor stuff, from the viewpoint of today. But not mild back then. Most of those early reworked Corvettes were done for the car magazines—where reader demands kept anything from going too far—or for the show circuit.

At the time, say the early and mid-Sixties, there were car shows done on a semi-pro basis. The top stylists in the field, Barris and Starbird, for two, did fully professional show cars which at the same time had to be actual cars. Backing them up, the farm teams as it were, would be the smaller and lesser-known shops, and guys working on their own cars with their own time and money. Fiberglass is simple to work with; why, you cut off the mistakes, grind down the places where the mistakes attach, mix up some more raw material and try again.

This was fun. Being a customizer was equal to being a drag racer: legitimate hobby that could turn into real money.

Just when the change came, I haven't been able to pinpoint, but if you check the cars in chronological order, you'll see a trend to wilder and wilder. What isn't in this book (thank goodness) are the other cars being shown to the public.

Extending the original theme wasn't enough. The public got tired of looking at just plain reworked cars and the shows had to become strange displays of the absurd. Four-wheel-drive bathtubs. Whiskey stills with twin superchargers. No kidding. Because the headlines and money went to things which weren't cars at all, there came a time when a vehicle which could actually be used on the public road wasn't worth putting in a show.

No real harm in the long run. If one can say the slack was taken up, it was taken up by drag racing.

In part, this was real racing. All racing has odd rules. In this case, because the Corvette

Above and below left: 1971 Custom Coupe, Sportwagon • Owner: Robert B. Schuller

Above, below center and right: 1970 Custom Coupe • Owners: Larry and Brenda Fournier

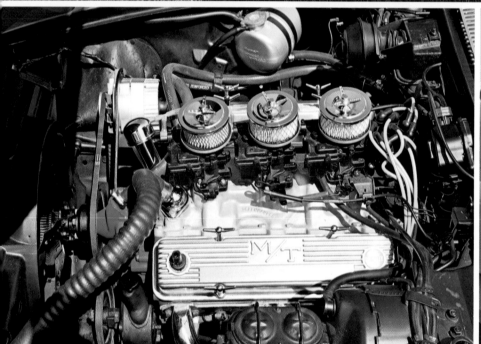

Page opposite: 1971 Custom Coupe • Owner: Mike Bigelow / Above and below: 1971 Custom Coupe, "P D Vette" • Owner: Sam Foose of Project Design

Below: 1973 Custom Coupe • Owner: Alan Fowler / 1970 Custom Roadster • Owner: Dave McQuinn

Above: 1972 Custom Coupe • Owner: Frank Bilotti / Below: 1972 Custom Coupe • Owners: Vic and Pat Feldon

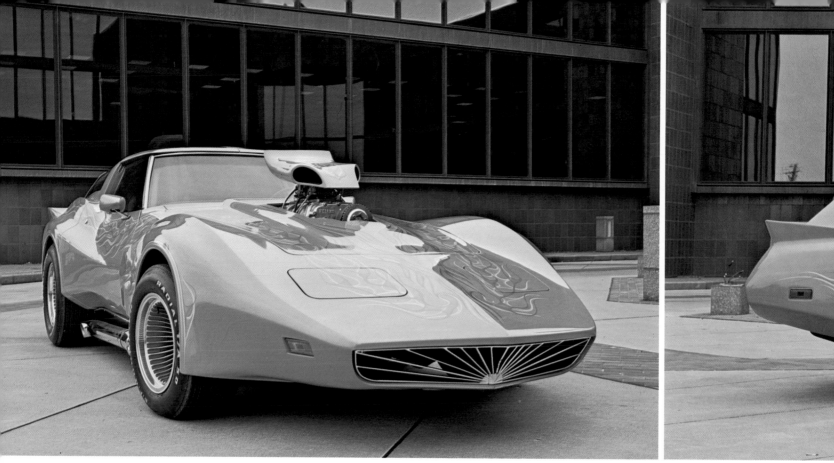

Above: 1974 Custom Coupe, "Draggon Wagon" • Owner: Jerry Pennington

Below: 1975 Custom Roadster, "Spyder" • Owner: Frank Milnay

Above and page opposite: 1976 Custom Coupe • Owner: James M. Phillips, Jr.

Below and page opposite: 1975 Custom Coupe • Owner: Lawrence Jones

Right: 1975 Custom Coupe • Owner: Ralph H. Eckler
Above and below: 1976 Custom Coupe, "Korky's Vette" • Owner: George Barris

was engineered to be a proper motorcar practically from Day One, it got the right engine in the right place, more in the middle of the car than your daily sedan. So the Corvette was a popular car for the quarter-mile. All forms of racing discovered the Chevrolet V-8 at about the same time and each branch helped the others, with more speed equipment than can be listed.

Some of this equipment showed up on the show circuit.

Some of it, probably more of it, ran on the street. Doesn't fit the usual definition of custom, maybe, but if the car is supposed to say something about itself and the man driving, then a street-legal '57 Corvette with fat drag slicks, traction bars, Hilborn fuel injector horns jutting through the hood and headers lurking beneath the doors, is a custom Corvette.

Road racing did the same, mostly with later cars. Fashions change, after all. First came flared fenders—fiberglass again made home customizing possible—and big tires on all four wheels, and sidemount exhausts and roll-over bars.

Were they all raced? Shucks, no. There

were some Corvettes running around town with GMC superchargers and bug-catcher intakes. There were Corvettes with fire extinguishers and electricity kill-buttons mounted aft of the driver's door, as required by the SCCA. Put it this way: There have never been more than perhaps a few hundred Corvettes in SCCA racing at any given year. There may have been a few thousand slalom racers and rallyists in competition at any given time. And any Corvette collector will tell you the hardest part of the hobby is finding an older Corvette that hasn't been modified in several ways. If these people weren't racing, and the figures prove they couldn't all have been racing, then it follows that most of the changes were made by Corvette owners who wanted their cars to go a bit faster, look a bit faster, in short, they wanted customized Corvettes.

Oh. I made that sound as if this is all over. It surely isn't. Right this minute and surely for years to come the Corvette owner will be able to buy the flares and scoops and wheels and tires, the complete list, to turn his or her car into a fire-breathing racer or replica convincing enough to never have to worry

about being challenged to a contest of speed.

Mention was made earlier of directions. Three come to mind.

The first was from Europe. Americans have long been in awe of European design, why I don't know, unless it's the human tendency to imagine that other people are different. (In Japan, by the way, there's a Morgan club more devoted than anything in England, right down to the deerstalker caps.)

When the Corvette became a serious and modern car, that is, when the Sting Ray appeared, several European coachbuilders did their versions of how the mechanical bits should be clothed. I believe they did this of their own free will, as compared with efforts done by the same design houses on contract from other American manufacturers.

That tells you something about how the Corvette was regarded in Europe.

These customs, for the most part, were neither as striking or as attractive as the original.

That tells you something about the original.

Second direction was practical. A freelance designer came 'round one day with an

interesting idea. A Corvette station wagon. There had been something of a fad for sports wagons, from Aston Martin and a commissioned job on a Mustang, so this seemed to make sense.

Nice work, too. The man planned to make kits, so any Corvette owner could extend his roof and enlarge the interior without making his car any bigger or less attractive.

I don't think he sold many. Nor have any others who have tried. Impracticality, in the sense of seating space or luggage capacity, has never been something Corvette owners worried about.

Point three is John Greenwood's Corvettes. Oh, I know, the expanded body sides and longer and lower nose and flared fenders and rows of air intakes and giant rear spoilers and all the rest are functional. They keep the car on the ground at 220 mph and allow it to function at top speed for twenty-four hours and give double the standard cornering power while meeting at least the letter of the rules . . . I don't care.

Greenwood's Corvette is the finest example of custom Corvette, a good design made better by accentuation, I've ever seen.

Greenwood Corvettes. A GT conversion on a 1977 Corvette (below center) and a GT Wagon (below).

The Greenwood IMSA car during construction (above) and at race debut (below) at the Glen, July 1977.

My Brother's Heart Remains Unbroken

When last we saw my older brother he had returned from his freshman year in college, reclaimed his Austin Healey and thus propelled my father into purchase of a Corvette. After that, my older brother became a conventional man and has since led a conventional life—that is, he went to work for a large corporation, married and had children, gave fleeting thoughts to driving in races but never became more than a fervent fan. He sold the Healey when he got married, bought an M.G. when he and his wife could afford it, traded that for a sports coupe, then a station wagon and, finally, material success having arrived in due course, he bought . . . a Corvette.

A 1975 Corvette convertible with the hottest-then small-block V-8, the four-speed stick and all options.

He is terribly proud of the car. We live on different coasts so I've never seen it, but ever since he brought his pride and joy home he's been telling me about the power, the speed, the air of brutal elegance, etc., and I've been acting the way we act when confronted with pictures of somebody else's children, i.e., polite but not too awfully involved.

Then I told him about this book.

Great! he said. Want to use some pictures of my car? Last of The Convertibles.

Frankly, I didn't speak frankly.
I was evasive.

Human nature. About the time I began getting out of the production car testing business, say late 1971 and early '72 until early 1973, modern cars went through serious troubles. Might even call them traumas.

This was the time in which all the tough emissions laws arrived. As (in my opinion) an attempt to defend against them by putting the blame on somebody else, General Motors decreed no GM engines would be required to burn leaded gasoline. This in effect banned high compression engines. Emissions were reduced, mostly because at least one of the noxious substances coming from tailpipes was

the product of efficient—right—efficient combustion.

So the high performance engine as we knew it in the Sixties went down the legal tubes.

It got worse. All cars produced for public sale in the United States had to be certified. This is an incredibly expensive and involved process. The rules require not just the basic car to undergo literally weeks of testing, but that every engine, transmission, final drive ratio, etc. be tested and certified in each of its possible combinations.

In the age of Supercars, the Corvette came with maybe eight engines, four transmissions and six or so choices of final drive, as a convertible, a coupe or a combination of both. You couldn't order any engine with any transmission (nor would anybody want, say, the ZL-1 racing motor with three-speed stick) but the total of combinations must have been close to forty or fifty.

Far as I know nobody has ever proved conclusively whether or not Chevrolet actually makes money from the Corvette. The company says yes, but there are some observers on the outside who believe the Corvette is there for prestige. Either way, if there are fifty models and it costs $10,000 to certify each model, you can't sell 50,000 Corvettes annually at competitive prices and pay the rent too.

Chevrolet did what all the other makes and models did; they dropped the lesser sellers in order to have the money to certify the more popular models. Thus you have stick shifts gone from the Mercedes-Benz line and on down the row.

The wonderful alloy blocks and supertuned small-block V-8's were at the time not the leading sellers. Worse, they were harder to certify because they were more efficient. Away they went, followed by the big-block engines, the wilder axle ratios, etc.

This didn't hurt the competition effort, because somehow the racing motors and

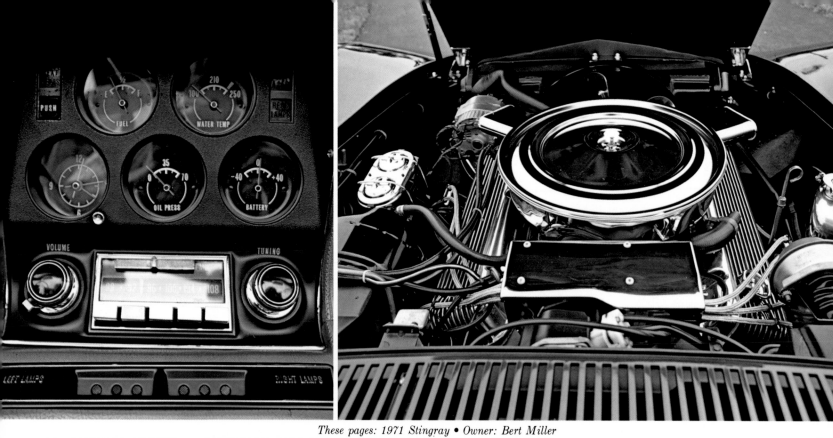

These pages: 1971 Stingray • Owner: Bert Miller

Pages preceding: 1972 Stingray • Owner: Kathy Russell

These pages: 1972 Stingray • Owner: R.D. Conners

Pages preceding: 1973 Stingray • Owner: Cleo Lampley

Above and below: 1973 Stingray • Owner: William E. Buie

Pages preceding: 1974 Stingray • Owner: David S. Filson, Jr.

equipment were always just behind the parts counter door.

The street versions took a beating. In my terms, anyway. First step toward becoming an historian must surely be adopting the belief that the era in which you deal was a wonderful era, far better than now—else why concern yourself with it?

Further, the insurance companies bullied the lawmakers and the carmakers into requiring and supplying bumpers—actually front body sections, as we'll see—which didn't get damaged at low speeds. The promise for this was less money spent on repairs and in turn lower car insurance. Pause for ironic laughter.

Corvette came through the last infliction quite well. The actual end of the body, as hinted, became a deformable section, springing right back into shape when dealt a small bunt. The reinforcements for larger blows are concealed inside, so the lines are sleeker than ever. The basic body hasn't changed, but the Corvette, as a result of all the above factors, has less power and speed, not quite as responsive an engine, more weight and more bulk. And the convertible body style was abandoned.

My big brother buys a new Corvette, see, and he expects me to get all aflutter over his new toy. I am being politely evasive because secretly I am assuming that his car is but a shadow of the Corvette from days gone by. My own '69 convertible, 104,000 miles and all, puts more horsepower on the ground than his engine develops at the flywheel. (Did I tell him this? Of course not!)

He outnumbered me, that is, despite my assumption that the Corvette of today was to the Corvette of the past as the Cobra II—right, I picked a gross example—is to the original Cobra, the public hasn't lost faith. Just the other day I read that all the 1977 Corvettes the factory can make have been sold.

Somebody was out of step.

For research, I borrowed a new Corvette. Two, in fact, one stick and one automatic, both with the current small-block V-8, 350 cubic inches and something like 200 bhp.

The out-of-stepper was me.

We are back at how they did it. Damned if

These pages: 1974 Stingray • Owner: Bob McDorman

I know how, but to sit in the '77 coupe is to be in a completely modern sporting grand touring car, while at the same time the emotional feeling is just like the feeling of sitting in that 1959 convertible on the first occasion my dad let me drive it.

Our concept of fashion may change, but dammit sirs, pretty girls are pretty girls. It's as clear and as intangible as that.

Nostalgia ain't what it used to be, somebody said, and thank goodness for that. The '59 was a bit of a truck. The clutch pedal was heavy, the gear lever was a big clumsy thing jutting out of the floor, demanding to be heaved back and forth. The steering wheel was spang up against your chest, the brakes took both feet, the ride was rough, the seating position bolt upright. Mind, I loved it. That's how sports cars were in those days, so I had no way of knowing any better if I had cared.

The new car was, well, refined. Driving position just right, and if you don't like it, you can put the steering wheel where you wish. Power brakes and steering, fine. Electric windows, FM radio, why not? All driving inputs are lighter, so the driver is free to be precise. Beautiful ride, while the increase in cornering power and traction under power and braking are so vast that people living in the past must thank their stars there were no skid pad tests in those days.

Still a fine looking car, almost as if the racing versions had been fitted for the road, rather than the reverse.

And it still draws the attention of the opposite sex.

Down the road in the automatic, cruising through the traffic, envied by all who see me, one eye on the tach and the other out the windows and the mirrors, a random thought cropped up: Too bad they don't have that torpedo back any more. My youngest will never know the thrill of riding back there.

Into the driveway. Out come the kids, led by my daughter, a mature eighteen-year-old young lady now. "Wow!" she shrieks, jumping up and down. "A Corvette. It's even the color I want."

Young and old alike, they never say in the car ads. The ad people know you can sell a

179

young man's car to an old man, while you
can't sell an old man's car to a young man.

So? Quick, name a car besides the Corvette
which is equally desired by your children and
your parents.

Acting like a parent, I gave the kids a ride
in a test car. Without me. Daughter driving,
little brother beside her and, yes, smallest
son vaulted into the luggage cubby between
the seats. How did he know that, do
you suppose?

They loved it. Slowly past their friends'
houses, then up and down main street of our
small town, to the drug store and back.

Oh yes. Performance. Nothing is more
relative than performance. From those early
days with the Stovebolt Six until now, the
Corvette has always been quicker than most,
a fraction less quick than a few, almost
always a more expensive and more
demanding few at that. The entire scale has
shifted down—again, my view of the
182 past—and the Corvette had shifted with it.

These pages: 1974 Stingray • Owner: Vernon Headrick

Turns out contemporary tests which I trust—shucks, I hired the man who performs the tests, in the most trustworthy case—put the Corvette just where a seasoned observer would expect. Your megabuck Porsche will edge the Corvette at the drags and in top speed, while the Corvette will show a pair of fat rear tires and a saucy flip tail to any sedan you're likely to meet. The more the government makes us change, the more we manage to stay the same, as the French say.

At one time I would have commented that the Corvette is a car of its time. Not strong enough. The Corvette is instead a car ahead of its time. Always has been. Regulations be damned, loss of open air motoring notwithstanding, the Corvette has always offered more than you could get from anybody else, for the money or the investment in bother.

My brother always did know best. Now I can tell him what I think of the current Corvette.

183

Above and pages following: 1975 Slingray

Owner: James B. Quayle III

Above: 1975 Stingray • Owner: Bob Brewer   Below: 1975 Stingray

wner modified • Owners: Charles and Yvonne Parker

Corvette People

Sonya is an attractive lady, with flashing eyes, a Junoesque figure, raven hair . . . and seventeen (at last count) Corvettes.

On the books, anyway. In actual fact, Sonya has only eight Corvettes in her own collection. They are personal favorites. The other nine are for sale. She keeps them all in a giant garage in an industrial center, where she tunes, polishes, rebuilds and restores a constantly changing stock in trade. She is a dealer in used Corvettes, a member in good standing of an informal league of Corvette collectors and dealers and, perforce, a ranking royalist in what must be the largest and broadest and in some ways most exclusive band of enthusiasts in a sport—being daffy about cars—which has no lack of enthusiasm or exclusivity.

Corvette people, to quote F. Scott Fitzgerald, are not like you and me. A paraphrase is needed. Corvette people are different beyond having more Corvettes than the rest of us do.

Exclusivity. The guys who took the pictures for this book are the best in the business. I know one of them personally. Nobody takes better pictures than he does. He is a painstaking craftsman, so respected that even Porsche owners smile and stand back when he sprays anti-sparkle stuff on their little gems.

Sonya and I were friends before she took the vow, so to speak, so she trusts me. Considers me almost a Corvette person. I mentioned our West Coast star photog to her during my research. Oh yeah, she said, the grapevine told her some person was asking about restored and rare Corvettes. Naturally, because they'd never dealt with the man before, never seen him at club events, because he drove a (clench) Datsun, their lips were sealed. Polite evasions were all he'd get from the inner circle. Claimed to be working on a book. Ha!

Oh my, I said. Listen. We are working on a Corvette book. I can vouch for the guy. He's super. Please take my personal word and pass your personal word on down the line. When you see how good the pictures are, you'll never forgive yourselves if your cars aren't there.

Okay, she said, and presumably the word went out. Far as I know, he never had another bit of trouble getting the proper cars and sources.

I'd estimate the spreading of the word took maybe half a day.

That the network works has surprised me, but it does work. Begin with a contradiction. Over here, a man with a Corvette for sale. Over there, a man who wants a Corvette of a certain year and style and options. The seller wants $4500 and the buyer will pay $6000. Sonya or one of the others in her group buys low, sells high and keeps the difference. How they do it? Simple. Only the insiders know both parties and neither party knows how to find the other without help, which isn't forthcoming.

To a lesser extent this works with some other marques as well. I mention it here, though, to illustrate the devotion and dedication generated by the Corvette since its inception. You can't have an elite group at the top of the pyramid unless you have a broad base of support, a large number of people keenly interested in something. That means you also must have something which generates interest, which the Corvette has surely done.

Lest the above sound as if I am opposed to fanaticism, let me hasten to say fanatics are the greatest sort of people. I mention Corvette's semi-pro ranks here because they could not be there without mass support. The actual topic is that support and how it came to be.

The formal record shows the first Corvette club began in 1956, when a new owner decided there should be a club. He collected eight other owners, they founded a club and away they went.

At roughly the same time, Chevrolet and Chevrolet's ad agency figured to generate some loyalty. They came out with *Corvette News*, surely one of the more self-descriptive titles ever. They also came up with—or he came up with them—a salesman by the name of Joe Pike. He became the insider, the Corvette fan and booster who had the influence and the budget to make sure the magazine reflected what owners wanted to look at and read about.

Currently something like 225,000 people receive *Corvette News*. The first club became a network of clubs. There are local chapters, having meetings and putting on their own events and just having fun with their cars. There's a council of clubs, which amounts to a national organization. The clubs are in touch with each other and organize inter-club and regional slaloms, area versus area challenges and the like. There are something like 300 Corvette clubs, with a large minority

The Thompson/Mahler Corvette, category winner at Daytona 24, 1970.

Pages preceding and right: The ARRC at Road Atlanta, 1972—Thomas Rizzo's No. 45 during qualifying, the massed start, John Greenwood entering the winner's circle. Above: The Gimondo-Trembley-Drolet-Belperch Corvette at Daytona, 1969. Below: Greder/Beaumont at Le Mans, 1973.

The Dave Heinz/Bob Johnson Corvette at Watkins Glen in 1971 (below), 1972 (above and right).

linked into the council and another good share being tied into another council.

(How that came about I don't know, but when you have people who believe strongly in something, you also have diverse opinions and groups break off or begin doing things their own way. A sign of life.)

Sounds pretty commonplace. Nearly every marque with scantest pretensions toward sport has an owner's club of some sort.

The comparison doesn't apply. For the owner of a make or model that never had vast numbers, or perhaps has died, membership in a club is required. If you're one of twenty-two owners of a Lea-Francis or whatever, you'd better be prepared with a list of all the other chaps in the country who might have a spare prop shaft on hand. Owners of orphans band together out of

196 mutual need of another kind.

No. 57 put up a string of GT victories, plus eighth overall at Daytona, fourth overall at Sebring.

The big clubs aren't usually too awfully active. A couple of hot workers at the top while the rest sit back and wait for the monthly bulletin to arrive.

Even so, Corvette owners are more involved than practically any other. Nor does commercial—that is, factory—backing have much to do with it. When Plymouth brought out the Barracuda, the factory people had noticed what Chevrolet had done for the Corvette owners, so the Plymouth opinion-molders created a Barracuda club, with local chapters and jacket emblems and a magazine and activities. Club lasted maybe one year. Nothing wrong with the car, nor with the people who bought Barracudas. It was just that the people who bought the cars weren't people who cared that much about the car for itself. (No offense intended. I own one myself and in fact still have the club

197

Rich Sloma (at top) during the IMSA Camel GT at Laguna Seca, '74.
Greenwood (above) en route to the SCCA Trans-Am Championship, 1975.
Greenwood again (below) at the Daytona 24 Hours of 1975 where his
Corvette was the fastest qualifier and put up the fastest lap as well but,
alas, did not stay the race and (right) at Road Atlanta for IMSA's
Camel GT, also in 1975, on the way to finishing fourth in the first heat.

Corvettes racing SCCA down south: At the top, moving out in Charlotte; above, Wayne Adams during the ARRC races at Road Atlanta in 1975. Below: The Jerry Thompson/Don Yenko sixth-overall-placing Corvette at the IMSA Camel GT at Mid-Ohio, June 30th, 1974. Pages following: The Levitt Racing entry driven by Steve Durst and Mike Brokman which finished seventh in the Camel GT at Pocono on August 15th, 1976.

member's badge on my jacket.)

No. Figure that 500,000 Corvettes have been produced since Day One. Allowing for better-than-normal care and maintenance, which could upset the normal life cycle of twelve or thirteen years for a car, there must be several hundred thousand Corvettes on the road. And there are better than one hundred thousand, maybe as many as two hundred thou, people who sign up for *Corvette News*, belong to one or more clubs, etc. I doubt any other model can beat that ratio of cars to active members unless you get into the stratosphere area of Ferrari or gut-level Lotus freaks.

Never mind the official history. My bet is

that Corvette became an emotional issue back when the first owners bought their cars and learned they had not followed the rules. They'd bought the domestic product. Came the V-8 and they had a sports car of humble origin. Worse, it did the sports car number better than the imports, while also winning at the drags and the salt flats.

The real band of sports car pioneers didn't feel this. The handful of car nuts who began all this were as much hot-rod builders as purists. They stuffed flathead Ford V-8's into Rileys, Buick engines in Mercedes chassis, raced Cadillac sedans.

The group which followed them came up with the old-chap nonsense. The second

group was in the majority when the Corvette appeared and so the Corvette never won full social acceptance. It didn't really get there until the social cachet of sports cars faded and sports cars became the property of the nut-ball racers and collectors (like you and me) it is today.

In fairness, hot rodders weren't any more keen on Corvettes than the sports types were, back then. Talk of brakes and cornering smacked of pretensions beyond one's station.

Buffeted by both sides, the Corvette people banded together. If the rules at road and drag club worked against the Corvette, the owners would write their own rules, stage

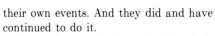

Above: Rick Hay during the Camel GT Challenge race at Mid-Ohio in August of 1976 Above left: Sam Posey en route to a third-place finish at IMSA's Camel GT, Lime Rock, September 1973.

their own events. And they did and have continued to do it.

Enforced camaraderie can be inherited. The first owners came to think of themselves as special and embattled. This attitude was passed along, bringing more clubs and more people into the clubs. By now the feeling of distinction is so engrained we don't notice anything. Naturally the Corvette owner takes better care of his car, parks it out of harm's way, goes in convoy to the races where he parks with his peers and cheers the racing Corvettes on to victory. Naturally. He owns a Corvette, after all.

There was a while back a plan in my mind to do sort of a Corvette honor roll, the names

Above and below: The Ford Smith and Phil Currin Corvettes at Mid-Ohio, June 1977, for the Camel GT.

Left and pages following: The Mancuso (De Pirro/Fyhrie/Greenwood) entry at the Glen Six Hours, 1977.
Bottom: The Motion Marketing Corvette (Mancuso-Coykendall) at the Watkins Glen Six Hours, July 1977.

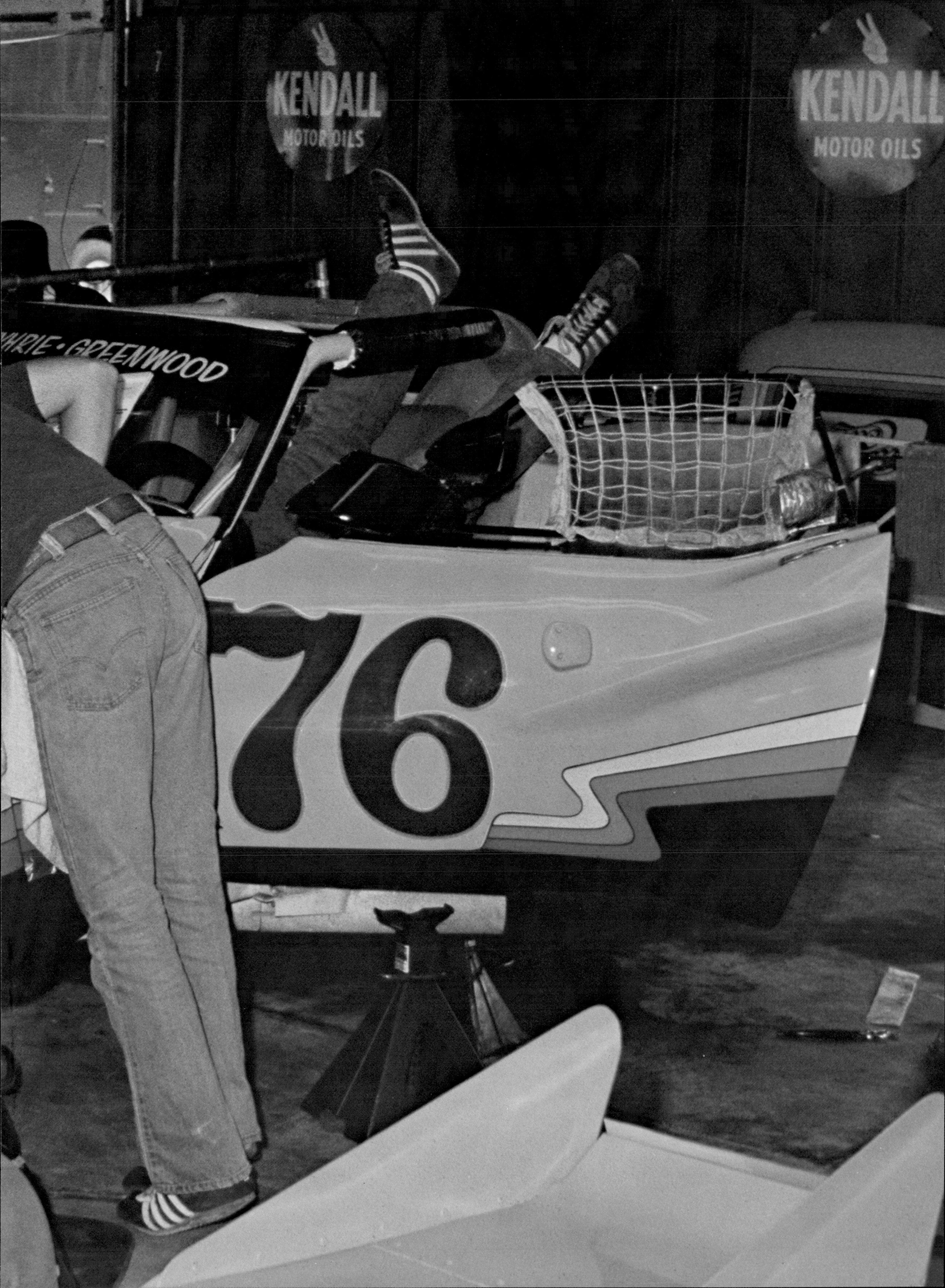
KENDALL
MOTOR OILS
KENDALL
MOTOR OILS
GREENWOOD
76

At the Watkins Glen Six Hours, 1977, the Corvettes of Bob Nagle/Nick Engles (No. 80), Alex Davidson/Kerry Hitt (No. 30), John G. Huber/Ron Weaver (No. 9,

In the "chute" between turns five and six (above) and storming into six's downhill left-hander (below).

and accomplishments of Corvette people during the past two-plus decades. Duntov at the top, surely. Mitchell as well. Then the guys who kept the brand going when sales fell in '55, the unsung heroes. Dr. Dick Thompson and the other racers like John Fitch who transferred from other makes because they believed in the Corvette concept. Allan Barker, winner of Lord-knows-how-many national championships. Drivers better known for other exploits, like Mark Donohue.

Start taking notes on a project like that and the notes grow beyond control and comprehension. At one time rallies—in reality, brisk-beyond-legality races with space-age time controls—were big in sports car circles. Turns out a Corvette won the national SCCA championship title 'way back. Who were the driver and navigator? How did they do it?

How fine a line should one draw? Dick Durant, an aircraft engineer out of St. Louis and a stocky man with gunfighter looks and outlook, won an SCCA title in a production Corvette. He damned near won the pure racing car title later, in a car he built around a Corvette V-8 with fuel injection. His car had a space frame he designed and built himself, covered by the scruffiest fiberglass body I ever saw. Whipped all the big-buck Can-Am leftovers at Daytona, of all places, until a $2 part let go. Not exactly a Corvette, true, but I used to assume that if Duntov ever saw Durant's car he'd love it.

Dick Guldstrand. A club racer, a professional racer and a good one. He learned so much about preparing Corvettes for competition that he was dragooned into business. Has a shop in Culver City and builds race and slalom cars to order. You pay your money and get as close to the championship in whatever you wish as your money and skill will take you. Great place to hang around except he's too busy to talk and the customers aren't always delighted to have somebody else peering at their speed secrets.

And so many more. The guy who went 190-something at Bonneville. Don Yenko, the Pennsylvania dealer/builder. The Europeans who bought and raced and won with Corvettes in the endurance races over there while the home folks were still trying to figure out what the Corvette would do. Travers and Coons, engine tuners par excellence. The hundreds of drag race contestants, the thousands of owners who simply dusted off the snobs at stoplight or slalom. My boss' wife, who used to come flying past me on the way to work, doing the ton or better, in her yellow '66 with full-race engine. All the other entrancing ladies who know how a Corvette makes *la différence* ever so much more *vive*.

Lord. You see where this is going to lead, namely an ever-widening circle. No way we're gonna have an honor roll. Everybody who ever drove a Corvette is just that extra bit special.

207

Keeping the Faith

Endangered species is an odd description for a car like the Corvette, a legend in its own time and so forth, but during the late Seventies the term was a perfect fit. The Corvette needed all the embattled friends it could get. The team responsible for the Corvette, as part of the Chevrolet Division and General Motors Corp., was embattled for reasons peculiar to the times.

First, the obvious. As we've seen in earlier chapters there were social and legal pressures that in effect took away the Corvette convertible and the big block V-8. The safety lobby, the insurance lobby, the new government agencies scratching for new measures as justification for their continued growth and influence, were naturally against big powerful cars, of which the Corvette was a prime example.

Further, General Motors itself was under siege. OPEC, rampant inflation, the fascination developed in trend-setting circles for anything imported — all factors beyond GM's direct control — put the automaker very much on the defensive. (It may have proved that GM doesn't run the country, but that would have been the sort of proof not accepted by people who need to believe the opposite.) In 1974, after what's been described as a shouting match, GM directors decreed a downsizing program. Cars would get smaller. They'd get more efficient. Or else.

Costs were cut. Budgets likewise, and what research money and time there was, was directed toward meeting the rules. The Corvette program wasn't destroyed, but it was reduced and called on the carpet. Creator Zora Arkus-Duntov once summed up his career scrapping with management for the Corvette in one word: struggle.

A third source of pressure was partially caused by the Corvette designers themselves. It was the enthusiast campaign, read here the press, for a new Corvette. Really new, as in NEW! Racy, mid-engined, and the engine should be something so exotic no other car had ever had such a thing.

This in a way began back when John Cooper beat the big front-engine Grand Prix cars with his little rear-engine car. The same thing happened at Indianapolis, followed by the major sports car races, the Can-Am, Le Mans, etc. Lots of racing fans got the idea that if backmotors were good on the track, they'd be equally good on the road.

Duntov never said no, not directly. Instead he pointed out that the low center of gravity, the extra traction from weight on the driving wheels, the better braking if weight transfer put equal weight fore and aft, all were fine for powerful racing cars. But on the road, there are problems with vision, egress, room for legs and feet and suitcases, isolation from noise.

Meanwhile there were various prototypes from the Corvette team's drawing boards and machine shops. Several were rear engined, more than one was powered by an exotic engine and on a couple of occasions the magazines said in so many words, "This is the new Corvette and it will be here in two years."

Which of course it wasn't. The prophets wrote in good faith; well, I know I did at least and I was one of those who wrote about the sure thing that never happened. We later learned the sources had spoken in equally good faith. What they didn't know is that the front vs. rear debate wasn't settled and wouldn't be until 1978. But that's in the next chapter.

Meanwhile, anybody who had experience with a De Tomaso Pantera, or who noted that when Porsche designed a big GT car, the 928, they reckoned that a front-mounted, water-cooled V-8 was the best way, should have been smart enough to work it out.

But we weren't. Instead, just about every time the model year rolled around with an evolved Corvette, the magazines shrugged and said here's the same old thing, where's the excitement?

All of which obscured the good work being done under fire.

Said good work is best seen by an annual review.

The 1976 model year was mostly consolidation. The Corvette came only as a coupe, with an engine choice of L-48, the standard version of the 350 V-8 rated at 180 bhp, or L-82, the same basic engine upgraded to 210 bhp. The engine was designed to run at higher temperatures, meaning more efficient combustion, but because of the higher temperatures under the hood a steel panel was added beneath the cockpit. And some trim was moved around, which happens every year.

The 1977 emphasis was on the interior. There was a new console, new heater and air conditioner controls. The steering column was shorter, making it easier to clamber in and out and the column now carried the dimmer and wiper/washer controls. There were still

Above: 1977 Corvette • Owner: Don Rood

Below: 1977 Corvette • *Owner: Chevrolet Motor Division*

Above left: 1978 Corvette Indianapolis Pace Car • Owner: Indianapolis Hall of Fame Museum   *Above right: 1978 Corvette Silver Anniversary Edition •*

Owner: Chevrolet Motor Division

Below: 1978 Corvette • Owner: Keith Campbell

the L-48 and L-82 engines and a choice of stick or automatic. Might mention here, though, that the optional engine was no longer high performance. It was the "high altitude" engine, just as back when stock cars were supposed to be really stock, the high compression cylinder heads were high altitude, or Denver, heads. Same illogic.

Double highlights in 1978. This was the Corvette's 25th anniversary so for this one year the traditional crossed flags emblems were replaced with 25th anniversary emblems. And the Corvette was chosen as pace car for the Indianapolis 500, resulting in a Limited Edition model.

Paint for the Corvette Pace Car replicas was two-tone, variations on black and silver with a red accent stripe separating the two. The interior also had silver trim. Decals proclaiming the pace car designation were supplied with, but not on, each car. The plan was to supply one car to every dealer, about 6000, and official count at the end of the year was 6502.

Collecting (not just cars but all manner of objects) was especially big at the time. I've read of owners scoring huge profits on the pace car replicas and even squirreling the cars away as investments. I can't vouch for truth here and I hope it didn't happen. Buying a car not to drive sounds silly.

The 1978 Corvette got a larger, fastback rear window. Better vision, less air drag and more stowage capacity behind the seats, which is of course all the stowage a Corvette has. With the extra room came a roll-out cover for the stuff in the bin, to keep it shielded from sun and prying eyes.

The L-48 and L-82 engines got their numbers juggled and California's ever-tightening emissions noose meant that state got the 350 engine with 10 bhp less than the 49-state base version. All the cars got larger fuel tanks, from 17 to 24 gallons. The company said it was for added cruising range, but I think it was so you wouldn't go through the pain of paying for a fill-up so often.

The 1979 theme was refinement. The emblems went back to crossed flags and lighter bucket seats, first offered with the limited edition '78s, became standard. The seatbacks now folded flat, the better to reach the larger rear bin, and the seat tracks were changed to allow the seats to go another inch forward.

Stick shift models got the softer shocks used with the automatics, closely followed by half a handling package. With either stick or automatic you could get the heavy-duty shocks from the gymkhana package, minus that option's stiffer springs. Same basic drivetrain: two versions of the 350 V-8, choice of transmission. The air intake system was revised for better cold starts and driveability and the cars with automatic came with lower (higher numerically) final drive ratio.

Speaking of collecting, in 1979 the Krause Auction people said the $550,000 paid by a Texan (who else?) for a turbine-powered

Corvette built by Andy and Vince Granatelli (ditto) set a world record for a car sold at auction. Since surpassed, I believe, but still...

The 1980 Corvette news was weight, lack of, a reduction of 238 lbs. There was a new bumper system, lighter top, hood and door panels, thinner glass for windshield and windows, aluminum in place of steel for parts of the frame, an aluminum intake manifold for the 49-state 350's and stainless steel exhaust manifolds for the 305 V-8 sold only in California.

In fact, the 305 was the only engine sold in California. At 180 bhp, it was rated 10 ponies less than the standard engine, and a whopping 50 less than that year's L-82. It was also the smallest displacement engine to find its way into a Corvette since 1961. Those were dark times indeed for California's faithful followers of the Plastic Fantastic. Poor devils.

The body got air dams and spoilers and a low profile hood and claims of lower drag, another subject becoming popular with all the factories. The 49-state automatics came with a converter that locked solid above 30 mph; less slip, less gas consumed. The sticks had lower, again read higher numbers, ratios in first and second gears, so there'd still be brisk take-off with a taller final drive. The government's imposed miles-per-gallon rules were also getting tougher.

The engineers unknotted the noose for 1981, or maybe it was a trade for previous sacrifices. All 50 states were allowed the 350 engine again, and they all could have stick or automatic but there was just one baseline engine. No high-performance version was certified under any name.

Engineering news was a fiberglass-reinforced plastic single leaf rear spring. Yes, it sounds impossible. What we mostly know about plastic is that it breaks if you bend it. But there are all sorts of plastic. The single leaf spring, available only on cars with automatic transmission and standard suspension, weighed 33 pounds less than the multi-leaf steel spring it replaced.

As another hint of things to come, the '81 engine was monitored by a black box. Marketing-coded Computer Command Control, the electronic marvel plugged into the carburetor, ignition and torque converter. It adjusted mixture and timing for optimum settings under all load and operating conditions, i.e. it fed the engine as much advance and as little fuel as the engine would take.

About halfway through the year, Corvette production was transferred from the old St. Louis plant to a sparkling new plant in Bowling Green, Kentucky. This led to some confusion. For a few months Corvettes were built at both places. They were supposed to be alike except the paints were different and weren't compatible, something to keep in mind if you need to touch up those gravel nicks. The change was needed, though, both because the new plant could make better cars and because new techniques and added

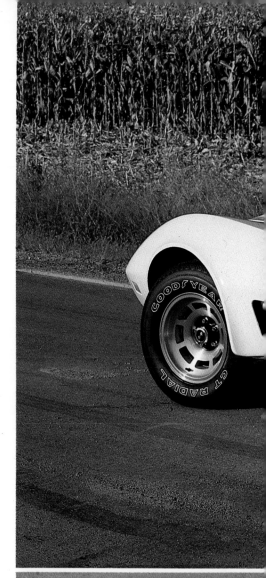

These pages: 1979 Corvette • Owner: Bob McDorman
Pages following: 1980 Corvette • Owners: Jerry and Bev Butler

Above: 1981 Corvette • Owner: Ken Torres

Below, left and right: 1981 Corvette • Owner: Roger's Corvette Center

Above: 1982 Corvette • Owner: Kathy McCarthy

capacity were going to be required in the future, nudge, hint.

The 1982 Corvette was the last of its generation, the final version of the basic package introduced in 1968. But there was more to the '82 than that. It was the old body, frame, and suspension, all right, but it was literally powered by the engine of tomorrow.

Fuel injection. Not the fabled fuel injection of 1957 but something different, done for different reasons. The formal name was Cross-Fire Injection, which sounds like what your ignition does when the plug wires get frayed. What the system really is, is two non-carburetors atop a dual intake manifold. These injectors meter the fuel as delivered under pressure, hence injection. Fuel is drawn from a carburetor by engine vacuum. The pressure approach is more positive, so to speak, and the mixture can be more closely controlled. Said control comes from another black box, again linked into the ignition and the transmission. The settings can be calibrated to pass the tests at this point, deliver optimum power at that point. The good old 350 V-8 got a higher compression ratio and longer camshaft timing, i.e. more power, back up to 200 bhp. There was just the one engine and one transmission, the four-speed automatic with locking torque converter on the top three speeds.

Because the '82 was known to be the last in

cross-fire injection

the series there was a standard model and a Collector's Edition, which had a lift-up rear window, at last giving direct access to the luggage. The collector car, a $4200 premium over the standard Corvette, also had different paint, special wheels and fancy little things inside.

There was no 1983 Corvette. Some pre-production models, the ones used for shows and demonstrations, were registered as '83s but officially the 1982 model run continued until October 1982, and the first new Corvettes were introduced to the public at large in April 1983, so under the odd rules of the auto business they could be — and were — billed as 1984's.

But the story's not over yet.

Two salient facts here.

One, the false predictions mentioned earlier were made in good faith. Chevrolet really did plan, at one time, to bring out the new car earlier than they did. But because of money and time and mostly because the Corvette was so popular, they kept on with the older version.

According to the factory's figures, there were 10,939 Corvettes built in 1961. The figure for 1971 is 21,801. And in 1981 the total was 40,606. During the 20 years, despite all the troubles, Corvette sales virtually doubled, then doubled again.

Same for enthusiasm. There are something like 700 Corvette clubs. There are formal and informal groups, approved and independent Corvette magazines. There are not only restoration experts, there are rival schools of experts, and rival national meets. All part of the sport.

Second point: below I have made a little chart. It contains the figures important to a car like the Corvette, as in curb weight as

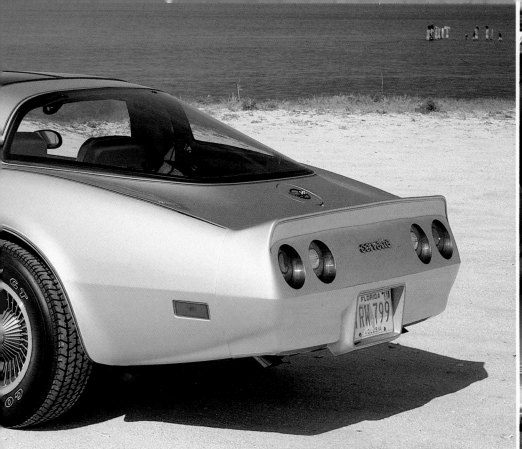

Owner: Jacqueline Steindl

tested, elapsed time for the standing quarter mile, how many miles per gallon. The figures come from *Road & Track*, which in my mind (true, I work there) does the best tests.

Model Year	Curb Weight (lb)	E.T. 1/4 mi (sec)	MPG
1968	3260	15.6	11-15
1973	3520	15.5	14.5
1976	3610	16.5	14
1977	3540	15.5	15
1978	3490	15.2	15
1979	3655	15.6	12
1980	3345	16	14.5
1982	3425	16.1	21.5

Now then. The 1968 test was with the 350 engine rated at 350 bhp. The 1973 car was an LT-1, the post-lead version rated at 250 bhp. Look at the weights, the times and the mpg for them compared with the 1982 car. Remarkable. Smog controls, crash-proof bumpers, all the dumb things that were supposed to ruin our fun, didn't. One could say we got a better Corvette. (Oh, yeah, the mileage in 1979. Ignore it. That was the result of a group test and the cars were flogged for hours at unprintable speeds.)

Our friends in the Corvette group, and Chevrolet and even General Motors, did a wonderful thing here. Against the odds, despite the pressures, they kept on building a true sports car when the rivals, for example the Jaguar E-Type and the Ford Cobra, went away.

They knew that the critics watch the waves and ignore the ocean. Public enthusiasm for buying cars may have waned, but the car nut's interest in performance cars didn't.

The Corvette guys kept the faith.

The New Generation

Numbers. Rolling down the highway in the late evening I had the sunset to my right, pitch dark to my left. The race track was disappearing in my wake; home, family, and a nice hot dinner were 150 miles down the road.

But right in front were the numbers. It was a great collection of information and a subtle form of insurance.

I was in a 1984 Corvette, the full-boat version with the Z-51 suspension and four-speed stick with overdrive on the top three. This Corvette was prepared, right down to a set of shaved Goodyear Gatorback tires.

But this was a state highway, broad and flat and not too busy, fine for covering miles but equally suited for those who wish to observe and collect. Because it was dark I couldn't tell who or what was behind those lights coming up from the rear.

Hence, the numbers. The fifth generation Corvette's instrument panel isn't what it used to be, even less is it like the row of dials one associates with racing cars. Now there are colored graphs, artfully curved for the speedometer, shaped like a dynamometer test chart for the tach. Centered between the graphs are digital read-outs, banks of computer-friendly squares and buttons. The driver/operator can punch up how far he has traveled, for instance, or how many miles until the car needs fuel, or the average speed this far into the trip, or the miles per gallon so far. And of course there are digits to supplement the colored curves.

This was fun. I settled into a prudent speed, slightly slower than the last car past me, and tuned the excellent radio to suit myself. Ditto the seat. Then I rolled off the miles while checking averages, all the better for telling me this Corvette, the best production racer on the market, was returning mpg in the twenties while loafing along at 2500 rpm.

Notice the concealed punchline: best production racer on the market.

I say that because this trip home from the track came at the conclusion of a comparison test of the leading contenders in the Sports Car Club of America's new class, Showroom Stock GT. SS/GT is the top of the heap, including cars like the Porsche 944, Nissan 300ZX Turbo, Mazda RX-7, Camaro Z-28 and Firebird Trans Am.

A comparison test was inevitable. I was invited on the grounds of previous racing experience and I had a wonderful time. Cars are better than ever; better than me one could say, seeing how I spun out three times and still didn't teach the young whippersnappers how it was done. The Corvette was better than the others, by several useful seconds per lap.

The instrument panel, though, was one of the items criticized. Digital read-outs and intriguing curved lines aren't suited for racing. If you have to think on the track, you're doing things too slowly and you have to think when you're looking at numbers. Dials aligned to give you needles straight up when all things are fine work better. What we race testers did, rather than decipher, was to rely on Chevrolet to have built a car that wouldn't overheat or lose oil pressure, and we shifted by keeping the tach curve in the yellow and out of the red.

The lap times proved that the fifth generation Corvette lived up to its name and heritage. And the drive home proved the instrument panel to be good for the sort of driving most of us do most of the time.

In short, the latest Corvette is a terrific car.

Heritage is the reason. The previous generation, the 1968-1982 Corvette, was a logical development of the '63-'67 Corvette, itself a carefully evolved replacement for the '56-'62 Corvette which in turn grew out of the original 1953 Corvette.

There were powerful reasons for Chevrolet to maintain this continuity of thought and design, not least of which was the car's continuing popularity.

There were also powerful reasons to do something really different, something exotic, to offer startling proof that America can design and innovate as effectively as the Europeans.

The world, the car world and the world at large, had changed a lot since 1968. Safety and efficiency had become political vehicles, while racing cars had become almost completely separated from road cars. A few factories,

1984 Corvette • Owner: Chevrolet Motor Division

depending on a unique look and a stunning sticker price, were building rear-engine road/ sports/GT cars. Chevrolet and Corvette designers had built a series of backmotor prototypes billed either as the next Corvette or as a possible next Corvette and the enthusiast press had happily gone along with the campaign.

The decision was made in 1978. There were many factors involved, but the real reason the fifth generation Corvette has the engine in front and the driving wheels in back is because General Motors decided to continue making the Detroit staple, the V-8 engine.

The Corvette design team started there. The Corvette is a performance car, a driver's car. It must be among the fastest production cars in the world or it has no reason to exist, indeed it probably would disappear if it didn't offer more performance than lesser, cheaper cars.

And it must appeal to, and be within financial

reach of, hundreds of thousands of buyers during its projected model run. And of course it must have an engine based on a mass-produced passenger car unit.

Now. It's possible to make small-engined, lightweight speedsters (Lotus Elan), or specialized big-engined hybrids (Ford Cobra), or exotic, high-performance GT's with multiple cams and carburetors (Ferrari 308). But the combination of high performance and low (relative) price add up to V-8 power, the cubic inches for which there are no easy substitutes.

It's a matter of scale, really. If a car has 200 or 250 horsepower, no matter how the power is developed, it must have a gearbox, drivetrain, brakes, and chassis to handle the power. Likewise, two people, their luggage, and amenities such as air conditioning must also fit into the package. Actual engine placement or displacement doesn't alter this, and as a result, powerful cars tend to be heavy.

Curb weight of the latest 308 Ferrari, for instance, is 3200 lbs. Just because the car gets 230 bhp from a four-valve, high-revving 3-liter V-8 instead of from a two-valve, low-revving 5.7-liter V-8 doesn't make it lighter. The Aerovette prototype was probably the closest the Corvette designers came to a genuine rear-engine Corvette. But chief designer Dave McLellan says now it was a 7/8 scale car, and even before scaling up to become a real car, the Aerovette weighed 3300 lbs.

None of this came as a surprise to the designers. But because there was so much to be decided, and one guesses also because there were emotional involvements here as well, the decision wasn't made lightly. There were in fact two parallel projects — one with engine forward, the other with engine aft — under way at the same time. Further, the design team rounded up all the Corvette's potential rivals, the 308, the De Tomaso Pantera, et al. and drove them to see what could be done. They concluded that they could use the race-based format to come up with a different Corvette.

But that wouldn't make it a better Corvette. So, aided by continued production of the V-8, they kept the established parameters and invested the engineering in a new generation car that was better, but not wildly different in principle.

Thus, the Corvette project was an illustration of automotive development. The first Corvette was a fiberglass body plunked atop a passenger car frame of the day, two parallel rails with cross members. The shape of a ladder, just as had been done for generations. Subsequent versions got independent rear suspension and the fourth generation evolved into a main frame with a subframe for the cockpit and the body around, instead of atop, the framework.

Car makers worldwide, meanwhile, had virtually declared the separate frame extinct. Modern cars have strong bodies that serve as their own frames, frequently with subframes for the front suspension and the engine.

The Corvette's fiberglass body made this impractical. (It's possible to make a unibody of plastic — like the Lotus — but the expense and bother aren't worth the cost on a mass-produced automobile.) So the Corvette team came up with what they call a uniframe, a term derived from unibody, surely. The uniframe is a three-dimensional structure of steel sheets welded together, a mix of the space frames and monocoque tubs seen in racing.

There's still a subframe, of sorts. The front crossmember carries the front suspension, engine and transmission. A tunnel/bridge runs back alongside the driveshaft to the differential. Abaft the differential is a carrier for the fiberglass rear spring and the rear suspension. The drivetrain is assembled, then goes beneath the uniframe plus body as a unit.

1984 Corvette • Owner: Chevrolet Motor Division

One cannot overemphasize the time and effort involved here. It sounds trite but the Corvette got the best of both worlds. A small, specialized company devotes all its time and resources to getting the new car just right... but its time and resources are limited. The mass producers have thousands of engineers and computers and wind tunnels... but they can't afford to take a design beyond acceptable. An engineering center responsible for scores of models built by the millions can't devote extra time to one design because it takes away from the others.

But the Corvette team had only one car, and General Motors gave Chevrolet permission to let the Corvette people do what needed to be done. They went over the design piece by piece, inch by inch, literally. Some of this we can appreciate. Because the lift-off roof panel flexed with the best of latches, there are bolts. And the roof stays in place. Because the

owners of special cars like mechanical things, the engine compartment is laid out like a show car, all the wires in place, color-coded, just so. We know other things indirectly. Suspension bushings are tuned for that fine balance between too firm, which transmits vibration, and too soft, which makes the steering feel vague. We'll never exclaim over the perfect bushing, but we do notice the smooth ride and the precise steering response.

And some things we'll never know, we hope. This is a complicated car. Hard to imagine doing the old body-off restoration number here. So the pieces are coated and isolated with a twenty-year working life in mind, that is, only the professional few will ever have to cope with the built-in intricacies of this machine.

Style is in the eye of the beholder, as we usually say when we're preparing to criticize. My intent isn't exactly that, but it is worth

mentioning that while the designers say they began with a clean sheet of paper, the new Corvette looks mighty like the earlier ones and a lot like the current Camaro, which is a lot like the previous Camaro.

Not entirely fair, that remark. What the resemblance mostly means is that the same bunch of designers were at the drafting tables in the styling studio when the clean sheets of paper arrived.

Also, because the public must be able to identify the car instantly, it makes sense to have it look something like the previous car. And then there was the government's edict concerning the average gas mileage of all cars from all factories. So the Corvette could be used to benefit the corporate average by having a new body as sleek and slick as possible.

For my part, the Corvette looks great with bright, strong, even metallic paint. It's less attractive in pastel or in flat paint, and from some angles I get the feeling the car went through the wind tunnel once too often. But then I liked Indy better when cars were iron and drivers were visible.

In sum, thanks to all those computer runs and stress tests, no part is larger or heavier than it needs to be. The fiberglass body and aluminum suspension pieces help here too. The fifth generation Corvette is both smaller and lighter than the model it replaces. Check the records for another time *that* has been achieved.

Back, now, to affairs of the heart, and back to the comparison test mentioned earlier.

A race track is a good place to meet a new car. The absence of drunks, stray dogs, farm wagons, mobile homes and radar allows the mind to concentrate wonderfully. A track is a high pressure (note I don't say crash) course in how a car works.

Working here applies in two senses. Under ideal but fair conditions the new Corvette has generated one g of cornering force. Outside testers haven't done this well but all agree the car corners with record grip. The engineers spent just as much time developing and refining transient response, what the car does when the driver turns the wheel. The car is as good in the slalom as it is on the skid pad: goes right where you aim, when you aim. And of course there's ample power always on tap.

The second sense of working is a matter of confidence. One can't get this from scientific measurements. Two cars may have equal skid pad and slalom results. They both go through the sweeping turn at, say, 90 mph. But one feels right, secure on the road, while the other seems on the ragged edge, poised to bite back.

The Corvette is the former. The sensation is of being securely slung within a framework of four giant wheels. You steer and shift and brake and mash the long thin pedal and the Corvette zooms around the track. When the car hits the bump at the entrance to the track's fastest corner, it goes light then comes back down, still straight. Not too worry, as they say.

The new generation car proved a fine highway cruiser and then did yeoman service around town between sporting drives in the mountains. Hard to imagine getting into serious trouble with this car unless the driver is so stupid or clumsy that the car's too good for him. The only drawback in daily use comes with the territory, that is, low cars are more awkwardly entered and exited than tall cars are. That aside, there wasn't much to fault.

For me, anyway. During the 1984 model year the engineers were told they'd gone too far in developing the suspension for the skidpad and slalom. Too stiff and too direct, the critics said. So the 1985 Corvette has softer suspension, both in the standard and in

the optional Z-51 versions. No loss on smooth roads, it turns out, and a better ride on poor roads.

The 1985 also gets more power, due to an eight-port fuel injection system replacing the dual throttle-body version. This means a more inclusive set of monitors and controls and that in turn means the power can be closer to the optimum more of the time. Rated bhp jumps from 205 to 235. Published tests (of a pre-production car, take note) show the '85 Corvette as the fastest true production car for sale in the U.S.

History never sleeps, or maybe it's progress that never stops. But in this case it's safe to predict that the fifth generation Corvette will continue in its present form for several years.

Above and below: 1984 Corvette • Owner: Chevrolet Motor Division

They'll refine it, but they won't make radical changes. Sure, if GM abandoned the V-8, presumably the Corvette would then come with a highly tuned or enlarged V-6, but seeing how the big sedans with V-8's are selling well — people like big cars, even if critics don't — we can expect more of the same understressed power the Corvette has delivered all these years.

Success stories are the best kind. The Corvette isn't what it once was. It isn't the underpowered country-club cruiser with side curtains, nor the raked fuelie that terrorized the drag strips, nor the bellowing big block that thundered to all those championships.

But the men who make the Corvette have always put the car first. Nobody in authority ever lost sight of what the car is and what it's supposed to do.

So. When I climb into the '85 Corvette it's not at all like my dad's '59 or my brother's '75. But when I strap myself into the seat, turn the key and hear the sound of sport and performance, I think, just as they always have, "Gosh! A Corvette! Wow!"

Pages following: 1985 Corvette • Owner: Chevrolet Motor Division

The Improved Breed

Image is the important thing here. Right, we've come to use the word in a negative way, as if an image was somehow at odds with the facts.

For the Corvette, it's not. The fact is simply that the Corvette is America's premier sports/performance/prestige car. Everybody knows the Corvette, what the car is and what it stands for.

We're dealing here with customizing and racing. In racing, the facts of Corvette's performance and advanced engineering are a starting point for the image and the image is based on advantage.

Customizing, in contrast to coachbuilding, began at the grass roots. Nobody knows, well, at least nobody can prove, who or what was first. As soon as cars were produced all alike in large numbers, though, owners wanted something different. They trimmed this, threw away that. We've had several schools of thought: lead sleds, TV spectaculars and café racers, but the theme has always been to go beyond the limits of mass production.

As seen in these pages there are many ways to go. The lucky, the talented, the industrious few may build stretched Corvettes with four doors, convert coupes into convertibles, add racing bodywork to road cars or do some of the above and add one or perhaps two turbochargers.

This is romance, not practicality. There are thousands of showrooms packed with four-door sedans. One can buy a convertible readymade from Chrysler, Ford, Renault or Volkswagen. Anyway, it's easier to restore an old Corvette convertible than to convert a new coupe. And as most of us know (to our regret), you can get plenty of tickets driving cars that won't go 200 mph.

But when it's a four-door Corvette, or a convertible version of the 1984 model, or when it has two or three times the power of the stock engine, you have something that's gone beyond the starting point. The better the starting point — in other words, the image — the better the result of the work.

The same principle applies in racing. Just about the time the first Sting Ray was introduced, the Sports Car Club of America switched from production classes based on engine size to classes based on performance potential. The dozen models that could be modified to go the fastest comprised the top class, the next dozen were the class below that and so on. Then the National Hot Rod Association and the American Hot Rod Association opened the gates to funny cars, dragsters wearing replicas of road car bodies.

This was professional racing. The idea was to make every car competitive, so more people would want to come and watch. In a way this detracted from the Corvette. There's little advantage to starting with a car having proper weight distribution, a strong engine, four-wheel independent suspension and disc brakes if everybody else is allowed to build and equip their cars in the same way.

True production Corvettes kept right on winning the production classes, while today built-for-racing Corvettes win the professional, silhouette and in-name-only classes.

We're back with the fact and the image. Racing cars aren't road cars. A funny car will hit 250 mph in six seconds, but that requires 2000 bhp and a racing-only aluminum-block Hemi V-8 (descended from but not a version of Chrysler's second-generation Hemi). It must be supercharged to two atmospheres and burn racing fuel, and only an engine designed for this punishment can take it.

Road racing rules require roll cages and fuel cells. You can't do that with a production frame. It's easier to build a frame from scratch, so now the sports and GT prototype series use kit cars: racing frame, brakes and suspension motivated by a production-derived engine.

The prototype class goes beyond even that. They're true racing cars and make no pretense otherwise. Thus they usually have the engine behind the driver, covered by aerodynamic shells. This is fair, close, exciting racing. Just because the Corvette, Jaguar, Ford or Porsche on the track isn't what you can buy doesn't make the rivalry any less fun.

The Corvette race car is thus a tribute to the Corvette road car. They run as Corvettes because people identify with the car, which brings the top teams and sponsors, all because everybody knows that Corvette is the car to watch.

Drag race legend Tom "Mongoose" McEwan in the Coors funny car.

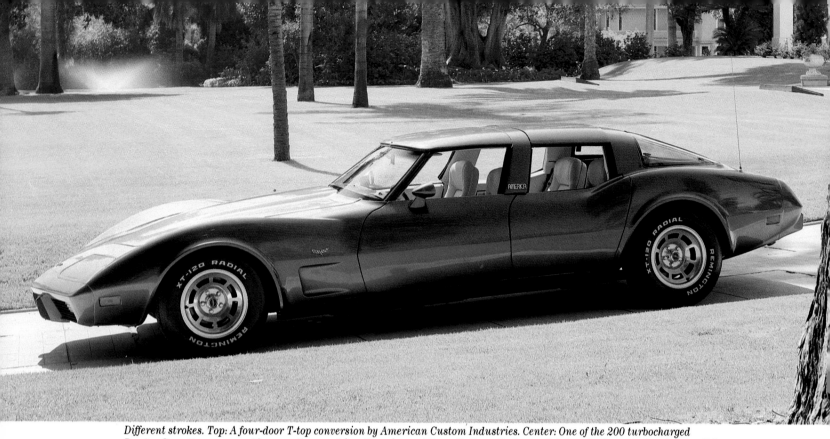

Different strokes. Top: A four-door T-top conversion by American Custom Industries. Center: One of the 200 turbocharged Duntov Corvettes, so named because the man himself engineered them. Bottom: Custom paint done by Corvette South on an '84.

Top: Eckler Corvette's 1980 "Daytona" with twin superchargers and body panels from an endurance racer. Center: A de-topped '84 from Convertible Specialists. Bottom: the same idea as performed by the racing shop of John Greenwood for Corvette dealer Roger Judski.

The name's the same. But the funny car of Jacenty & Zeinert, left, and Larry Baines' "Kentucky Gambler," right, have aluminum Black Hemi V-8's. The GTP Corvette, opposite, uses a turbocharged V-6 in a Lola chassis. It's a Chevrolet product, but it isn't the Corvette of tomorrow.

Road racers stick closer to the mark. The Dingman Brothers car, above, and the appropriately painted Canary Racing car, below, ran the 1984 24 Hours of Daytona. The Auriga Racing car, no. 26, led the pack in the Miami Grand Prix. All three have racing frame, suspension and brakes but they are powered by Corvette engines and their bodies at least appear to be Corvette panels with spoilers, wings, scoops and all the other downforce-producers added on.

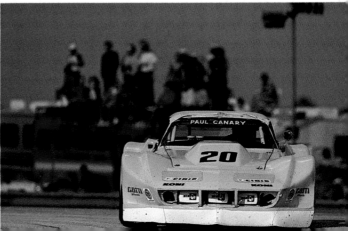

Corvette Specifications 1953-1984

ENGINES

	Cubic Inches	Bore & Stroke	C.R.	Gross bhp @ rpm	Model Years Offered
SIXES	235	3 9/16″ x 3 15/16″	8.0	150 @ 4200	53 54
	235	3 9/16″ x 3 15/16″	8.0	155 @ 4200	55
SMALL BLOCK V-8'S	265	3 3/4″ x 3″	8.0	195 @ 5000	55
	265	3 3/4″ x 3″	9.25	210 @ 5200	56
	265	3 3/4″ x 3″	9.25	225 @ 5200	56
	283	3 7/8″ x 3″	9.5	220 @ 4800	57
	283	3 7/8″ x 3″	9.5	245 @ 5000	57 58 59 60 61
	283	3 7/8″ x 3″	9.5*	250 @ 5000	57 58 59
	283	3 7/8″ x 3″	9.5	270 @ 6000	57 58 59 60 61
	283	3 7/8″ x 3″	10.5*	283 @ 6200	57
	283	3 7/8″ x 3″	9.5	230 @ 4800	58 59 60 61
	283	3 7/8″ x 3″	10.5*	290 @ 6200	58 59
	283	3 7/8″ x 3″	11.0*	275 @ 5200	60 61
	283	3 7/8 x 3″	11.0*	315 @ 6200	60 61
	305	3 47/64″ x 3 31/64″	8.6	180 @ 4200**	80
	327	4″ x 3 1/4″	10.5	250 @ 4400	62 63 64 65
	327	4″ x 3 1/4″	10.5	300 @ 5000	62 63 64 65 66 67 68
	327	4″ x 3 1/4″	11.25	340 @ 6000	62 63
	327	4″ x 3 1/4″	11.25*	360 @ 6000	62 63
	327	4″ x 3 1/4″	11.25	365 @ 6200	64 65
	327	4″ x 3 1/4″	11.25*	375 @ 6200	64 65
	327	4″ x 3 1/4″	11.0	350 @ 5800	65 66 67 68
	350	4″ x 3 31/64″	10.25	300 @ 4800	69 70
	350	4″ x 3 31/64″	11.0	350 @ 5600	69 70
	350	4″ x 3 31/64″	11.0	370 @ 6000	70
	350	4″ x 3 31/64″	8.5	270 @ 4800	71 72
	350	4″ x 3 31/64″	9.0	330 @ 5600	71 72
	350	4″ x 3 31/64″	8.5	195 @ 4400**	73 74
	350	4″ x 3 31/64″	9.0	250 @ 5200**	73 74
	350	4″ x 3 31/64″	8.5	165 @ 3800**	75 76 77
	350	4″ x 3 31/64″	9.0	205 @ 4800**	75 76 77
	350	4″ x 3 31/64″	8.5	180 @ 4000**	77
	350	4″ x 3 31/64″	9.0	210 @ 5200**	77
	350	4″ x 3 31/64″	8.2	185 @ 4000**	78
	350	4″ x 3 31/64″	9.0	220 @ 5200**	78
	350	4″ x 3 31/64″	8.2	195 @ 4000**	79
	350	4″ x 3 31/64″	9.0	225 @ 5200**	79
	350	4″ x 3 31/64″	8.2	190 @ 4400**	80
	350	4″ x 3 31/64″	9.0	230 @ 5200**	80
	350	4″ x 3 31/64″	8.2	190 @ 4200**	81
	350	4″ x 3 31/64″	9.0*	200 @ 5200**	82
	350	4″ x 3 31/64″	9.0*	205 @ 4300**	84
MARK IV V-8'S	396	4 3/32″ x 3 49/64″	11.0	425 @ 6400	65
	427	4 1/4″ x 3 49/64″	10.25	390 @ 5400	66 67 68 69
	427	4 1/4″ x 3 49/64″	11.0	425 @ 6400	66
	427	4 1/4″ x 3 49/64″	10.25	400 @ 5400	67 68 69
	427	4 1/4″ x 3 49/64″	11.0	435 @ 5800	67 68 69
	427	4 1/4″ x 3 49/64″	12.5	430 @ 5200	69
	454	4 1/4″ x 4″	10.25	390 @ 4800	70
	454	4 1/4″ x 4″	12.25	465 @ 5200	70
	454	4 1/4″ x 4″	8.5	365 @ 4800	71 72
	454	4 1/4″ x 4″	9.0	425 @ 5600	71
	454	4 1/4″ x 4″	9.0	270 @ 4400**	73 74

*fuel injected **net horsepower with emission controls

DIMENSIONS AND WEIGHTS

Year	Length (ins.)	Width (ins.)	Height (ins.)	Wheelbase (ins.)	Front track (ins.)	Rear track (ins.)	Curb weight (lbs.)	Weight distribution front/rear (%)
1953	167.0	72.0	52.1	102.0	57.0	59.0	2850	53/47
1954	167.0	72.0	52.1	102.0	57.0	59.0	2850	53/47
1955	167.0	72.0	52.1	102.0	57.0	59.0	2850	53/47
1956	168.0	70.5	52.0	102.0	57.0	59.0	2880	52/48
1957	168.0	70.5	52.0	102.0	57.0	59.0	2880	52/48
1958	177.2	72.8	52.4	102.0	57.0	59.0	3080	53/47
1959	177.2	72.8	52.4	102.0	57.0	59.0	3080	53/47
1960	177.2	72.8	52.4	102.0	57.0	59.0	3080	53/47
1961	177.2	72.8	52.4	102.0	57.0	59.0	3080	53/47
1962	177.2	72.8	52.4	102.0	57.0	59.0	3080	53/47
1963	175.2	69.2	49.6	98.0	56.8	57.6	3130	48/52
1964	175.2	69.2	49.6	98.0	56.8	57.6	3130	48/52
1965	175.2	69.2	49.6	98.0	56.8	57.6	3130	48/52
1966	175.2	69.2	49.6	98.0	56.8	57.6	3130	48/52
1967	175.2	69.2	49.6	98.0	56.8	57.6	3130	48/52
1968	182.5	69.0	47.8	98.0	58.7	59.4	3280	49/51
1969	182.5	69.0	47.8	98.0	58.7	59.4	3280	49/51
1970	182.5	69.0	47.8	98.0	58.7	59.4	3280	49/51
1971	182.5	69.0	47.8	98.0	58.7	59.4	3280	49/51
1972	182.5	69.0	47.8	98.0	58.7	59.4	3280	49/51
1973	182.5	69.0	47.8	98.0	58.7	59.4	3280	49/51
1974	185.5	69.0	48.0	98.0	58.7	59.5	3530	48/52
1975	185.5	69.0	48.0	98.0	58.7	59.5	3530	48/52
1976	185.5	69.0	48.0	98.0	58.7	59.5	3530	48/52
1977	185.2	69.0	48.0	98.0	58.7	59.5	3534	48/52
1978	185.2	69.0	48.0	98.0	58.7	59.5	3495	47/53
1979	185.2	69.0	48.0	98.0	58.7	59.5	3655	48/52
1980	185.3	69.0	48.1	98.0	59.0	59.0	3334	48/52
1981	185.3	69.0	48.1	98.0	58.7	59.5	3282	48/52
1982	185.3	69.0	48.1	98.0	58.7	59.5	3345	46/54
1984	176.5	71.0	46.7	96.2	59.6	60.4	3117	51/49

PRODUCTION AND SALES

Year	CALENDAR YEAR Sales	CALENDAR YEAR Production	MODEL YEAR PRODUCTION Total	MODEL YEAR PRODUCTION Coupe	MODEL YEAR PRODUCTION Convertible	Percent Coupes
1953	183	300	300		300	
1954	2,780	3,265	3,640		3,640	
1955	1,639	700	700		700	
1956	4,012	4,987	3,467		3,467	
1957	6,904	7,330	6,339		6,339	
1958	8,821	9,298	9,168		9,168	
1959	9,299	9,088	9,670		9,670	
1960	11,374	12,508	10,261		10,261	
1961	11,668	11,410	10,939		10,939	
1962	15,240	15,726	14,531		14,531	
1963	22,115	23,632	21,513	10,594	10,919	49.2
1964	19,908	19,892	22,229	8,304	13,925	37.3
1965	26,171	27,700	23,562	8,186	15,376	34.7
1966	24,754	24,939	27,720	9,958	17,762	35.9
1967	23,475	23,775	22,940	8,504	14,436	37.1
1968	29,874	32,473	28,566	9,936	18,630	34.8
1969	24,791	27,540	38,762	22,130	16,632	57.2
1970	22,776	22,586	17,316	10,668	6,648	61.6
1971	25,364	26,844	21,801	14,680	7,121	67.3
1972	26,652	27,004	27,004	20,496	6,508	75.5
1973	29,661	32,616	34,464	25,520	4,943	83.8
1974	29,750	33,869	37,502	32,873	5,472	87.6
1975	40,607	45,966	38,461	33,832	4,629	88
1976	41,673	47,425	46,558	46,558		
1977	42,571	46,345	49,213	49,213		
1978	42,247	48,522	46,776	46,776		
1979	38,631	48,568	53,807	53,807		
1980	36,507	44,190	40,614	40,614		
1981	29,039	27,990	40,606	40,606		
1982	22,477	22,838	25,407	25,407		
1984	11,535*	13,953*				

*through May 1984

SERIAL NUMBERS

Year	Designation	Beginning	Ending	Notes
1953	E53F	-001001	-001300	
1954	E54S	-001001	-004640	
1955	E55S or VE55S	-001001	-001700	
1956	E56S	-001001	-004467	
1957	E57S	-100001	-106339	
1958	J58S	-100001	-109168	
1959	J59S	-100001	-109437	
1960	00867S	-100001	-110261	
1961	10867S	-100001	-110939	
1962	20867S	-100001	-114531	
1963	30837S or 30867S	-100001	-121513	
1964	40867S or 40837S	-100001	-122229	
1965	194375S or 194675S	-100001	-123564	
1966	194676S or 194376S	-100001	-127720	
1967	194677S or 194377S	-100001	-122940	
1968	194378S or 194678S	-400001	-428566	
1969	194379S or 194679S	-700001	-738762	
1970	194370S or 194670S	-400001	-417316	
1971	194371S or 194671S	-100001	-121801	
1972	1Z37Y2S	-500001	-527004	
1973	1Z37Y3S	-400001	-438464	
1974	1Z37J4S	-400001	-437502	
1975	1Z37J5S	-400001	-438465	
1976	1Z37J6S	-400001	-446558	
1977	1Z37L7S	-400001	-449213	
1978	1Z87L8S	-400001	-440274	Standard
	1Z87L8S	-900001	-906502	Pace Car
1979	1Z8789S	-400001	-453807	
1980	1Z878AS	-400001	-440614	
1981	1G1AY8764BS	-400001	-431611	St. Louis
	1G1AY8764B5	-100001	-108995	Bwlng Grn
1982	1G1AY8764C5	-100001	-118648	Standard
	1G1AY0781C5	-100001	-106759	Collector
1984	1G1AY0781E5	-100001		

In 1955 the V-8's bore the VE55S designation. Beginning in 1963 the digits "37" indicate the coupe, "67" the convertible, with the first entry each year indicating the first car off the line. In 1972 the designation was revised as follows: "1" for Chevrolet; "Z" for Corvette; "37" for body style; "Y" for the 454 engine (the 350 carries the letter "J"); "2" for model year 1972; "S" for St. Louis factory manufacture. In 1981, a new federal law required serial number designations to include the manufacturer and the country in which the car was manufactured. These numbers translate as follows: "1" for U.S.; "G" for G.M.; "1" for Chevrolet; "A" for manual belts (no passive restraints); "Y" for Corvette; "87" for a coupe and "07" for a hatchback.

Notes and Photo Credits

The Corvette emblem, vintage 1958, is reproduced on our title page, photographed by Roy Query. The 1960 roadster on our contents page is from the collection of Bill Locke, photographed by Richard A. Brown. Pages 24-27: photographs by L. Scott Bailey. The other photographs accompanying the Bill Mitchell story are from the collection of Mr. Mitchell and the archives of General Motors Corporation. Pages 30-31, 38-39, 42-43, 46-47, 55, 60-61 below, 62-63 above, 68-69, 70-71, 74-75, 78-79, 82-83, 84-85, 94 above, 95 above, 98-99, 102-03, 104-05, 116-17, 118-19, 120-21 above, 122-23, 124-25, 132-33 below, 136 above, 138-39 below, 140-41, 144-45, 146 above, 147 above, 153, 155 below, 156-57 below, 164-65, 168-69, 170-71, 172-73, 174-75, 176-77, 184-85, 186-87, 188-89 above, 108-09, 210-11 above: photographs by Rick Lenz. Pages 32-33, 40-41, 44-45, 49, 56-57, 61 above, 62 below, 64-65, 72-73, 76-77, 80-81, 86-87, 94-95 below, 96-97, 120-21 below, 136 below, 160-61 above, 166-67, 188-89 below: photographs by Richard A. Brown. Pages 34-35, 36-37, 48, 50-51, 54, 60 above, 88, 89, 90, 91, 92, 93, 126-27, 128, 129, 130, 131, 132 above, 133 above, 134, 135, 137, 138-39 above, 142, 143, 146 below, 147 below, 148, 149, 150-51, 152, 154, 163 above, 178-79, 182-83, 203 above, above center and below, 212 above, 212-13 below, 214-15 above and below, 216-17, 218 above and below, 219 above, center and below, 220-21, 222-23, 224, 225, 226-27, 227, 228-29, 230-31, 232-33, 234, 235, 236, 237 top left and top right: photographs by Roy Query. Pages 52-53, 58-59, 180-81: photographs by Stan Grayson. Page 66 above and center: photographs by Dean Batchelor, courtesy of *Road & Track*. Page 66 below: photograph by Dwight Pelkin. Pages 100 above left, 100-01 above center and center, 110-11: photographs by Stan Rosenthall, courtesy of Motortext Incorporated. Pages 100-01 center, 101 above right, 106-07 below, 114-15: photographs by Dave Arnold. Pages 106-07 above, 192, 193: photographs by J. J. Mollit. Pages 108-09, 196-97 above: photographs by Geoffrey Goddard. Page 160 above and below: courtesy of George Barris. Pages 112, 113, 163 center and below, 198 below, 202-03 below, 203 below center, 204-05, 206-07 above and below: photographs by Bill Stahl. Pages 190-91, 194 above and below, 198 below: photographs by Pete Biro. Pages 195, 197 below, 198 above and center, 198-99 center, 199 above, center and below, 200-01, 202-03 above: photographs by Bill Oursler. Pages 198-99: photographs by Borman E. Brust. Pages 210-11 below, 213 above: courtesy of General Motors Corp. Page 237 center, below left and below right: photographs by Rich Chenet. We wish to thank World West Aviation Corp. of Van Nuys and Burbank Studios, Burbank, California for providing the locations for the photos on pages 78-79 and 119 respectively.